THE ULTIMATE
DUTCH·OVEN
COOKBOOK

THE ULTIMATE
DUTCH·OVEN
COOKBOOK

THE BEST RECIPES ON THE PLANET
FOR EVERYONE'S FAVORITE POT

EMILY AND MATT CLIFTON, Authors of *Cork and Knife*

PAGE STREET
PUBLISHING CO.

PAGE STREET
PUBLISHING CO.

TO THOSE WE LOVE, NEAR AND FAR.
YOU KNOW WHO YOU ARE.

TABLE OF CONTENTS

INTRODUCTION

Imagine, for the purpose of this introduction, that you've been shipwrecked on a desert island. This island, magically, has every food ingredient you could possibly ask for—whether you're an omnivore, vegetarian, vegan or pescatarian—but you were only able to grab one kitchen item from your ship before it went down. You have one single piece of cookware with which you now need to cook anything you can imagine.

If you chose a Dutch oven, then congratulations! This book is for you. (That was our choice, too.)

The Dutch oven that you've triumphantly dragged onto the island shore is the multitasking hero of the kitchen. It's equally at home on the stovetop or in the oven. It's sturdy, with thick walls and base that retain heat and guarantee even, steady cooking. It has a heavy, tight-fitting lid that will seal in moisture for those long, slow braises or trap steam to keep a loaf of bread soft during its oven-spring stage and help create a shiny, crisp crust. Those tall walls keep hot liquids in, making it a great choice for deep frying or for recipes where you just need a high volume to work all the ingredients together. It's roomy enough to cook an entire family meal and have leftovers for days.

The original cooking pots were designed to cook dishes over an open fire, either suspended by a handle or standing on feet. This became the Dutch oven early in the 18th century when the Dutch methods for brass casting—using sand for the finest results—were used on iron to make a cheaper pot. The idea of a sturdy pot with a lid is so universal that it's no surprise that you'll find it under different names, depending on the shape, size and where you live. You might find them under the name *braiser* (usually a wide, shallow pot), *cocotte* (often reserved for smaller, individual-sized ovens) or, outside the United States, casserole dish. (*Casserole* is a general international term that fits many of the stews and other recipes we include in this book.)

Most modern Dutch ovens are still made of cast iron—why mess with a good thing?—often with the one modern concession of an enameled surface. This makes for easier maintenance and also renders them nonreactive to acidic foods. You can also find versions in copper, other metals and ceramic. (Note: Some, but not all, ceramic pots are suitable for both stovetop and oven cooking.)

As for size, you'll find them listed by volume (usually by quarts in the U.S.). They range from 1 quart (1 L) for serving one or two people all the way up to over 10 quarts (10 L) for a huge gathering. We've found that something in the range of a 5- to 7-quart (5- to 7-L) oven is the most useful size for most dishes that serve six to eight people. That's the size we used to cook most of the recipes in this book.

There are fewer options for shape: Your choices are generally round or oval. There's not a lot of reasons to choose one over the other except for personal preference, but the oval type can be more flexible when it comes to braising a larger cut of meat.

When so much in our modern kitchens tends to value speed and convenience and automated methods for whipping up something quick, the Dutch oven, a piece of cookware essentially unchanged for centuries, hearkens back to classic techniques. It excels in low, slow cooking, bringing to the kitchen the pleasure of taking the time to do something right while also being a beautiful piece of cookware that you can bring to the table. And if you treat it well, it'll last several generations.

Just a quick note on maintenance while we're talking about it: If you have an enameled Dutch oven, there's minimal care involved. Don't use metal tools to scrape at the surface—stick to wooden or plastic tools—and use only non-scratch kitchen scrub sponges to clean it.

For a non-enameled cast-iron pot, treat it as you would a cast-iron skillet. Unless your pot comes seasoned, you'll want to season it by following the manufacturer's recommendations; usually this involves baking on a thin coat of oil. This ensures you start with a nonstick coating and helps prevent rusting. Frequent use of the Dutch oven is its own seasoning process. Always, always hand wash Dutch ovens—never use the dishwasher.

The Dutch oven is a skillet, a stockpot and a saucepan all in one. It will handle almost any recipe you care to cook in it, and, with the lid on in a low oven, is the perfect vessel to reheat leftovers. It doesn't require complicated instructions. You can invest in a beautiful top-of-the-line Dutch oven from a prestigious brand and have an heirloom-quality piece of cookware, but you don't have to break the bank to get ahold of a high-quality Dutch oven—many manufacturers offer excellent cast-iron or enameled versions for under $100. There's a reason why it's frequently the top choice on wedding registries!

If you didn't pick a Dutch oven as your desert island choice, please come on over and share ours. There's plenty of room in the pot.

MEASUREMENT AND INGREDIENT NOTES

We use both large and medium Dutch ovens in this book. A medium Dutch oven is approximately 4 to 6 quarts (4 to 6 L). Anything above 6 quarts (6 L) is large.

We only use kosher salt (not table salt) for cooking, but brands of kosher salt vary a lot in density (and therefore, the saltiness of a specified volumetric amount). Our measurements are for the Diamond Crystal brand; if you use Morton's, you can approximately halve any volumetric measurement, such as a tablespoon. If you weigh your salt, there should be no difference. As always, if you're adding salt to taste, start with a little and see how you go. Don't be afraid to differ from our suggested amounts: Your palate is the boss.

Matt & Emily

MOUTHWATERING BRAISES

We're starting the book with a chapter on braising, as it's with this cooking process that the Dutch oven shows its indispensability. The braising technique is, you might say, the meat and bones of this kind of cooking pot.

The general technique of braising is twofold. The central ingredient—often a tough cut of meat—is first dry-seared. Browning the ingredients creates a residue, or *fond*, on the bottom and sides of the pot, which is deglazed with wine or stock to create a flavorful braising liquid, eventually developing into a rich, finished sauce. The pot's heavy, heat-distributing bottom and its tight-fitting lid are both essential to a successful braise.

After searing, braises are cooked at a relatively low temperature, with a moderate amount of liquid, and for long enough to break down any toughness in the protein. Depending on what you're making, a braise can take half a day—as with our Osso Buco (page 27)—or just a few minutes, such as with our Hondashi and Sake–Braised Kabocha Squash (page 48). However, most recipes require an investment of time and a bit of forward planning. The good news is, once you've got the pot in the oven, you can generally leave it alone for much of the cooking time.

Braising is one of the best ways to transform a tough, inexpensive cut of meat into an elegant dish. A lamb shoulder, bundled with collagen and muscle, demands to be cooked low and slow, but once properly braised, it yields a rich, meltingly tender result (see the Slow-Braised Lamb Shoulder and Potatoes with Yogurt-Mint Sauce on page 31). Pot roasts and briskets belong in this category. Braising isn't always about meat, though, and we'll show you some vegetable braises, such as Moroccan-Spiced Eggplant and Chickpeas (page 44) that will demonstrate the versatility of this technique.

Braising is, at its core, an act of magical transformation, and a sturdy, sealed Dutch oven is the perfect vessel to pull off this alchemy.

SOY AND RED WINE—BRAISED SHORT RIBS

WITH PICKLED RED CABBAGE

We've been making beef short ribs for just about as long as we've owned a Dutch oven, and some version of this recipe is always on rotation. At the butcher, look for ribs with thick, well-marbled meat, but without too much fat on top. We use English ribs that are cut parallel to the bone, though you could also use thinner flanken ribs. The acidity in red wine makes a perfect base for the braising liquid, but we can't resist adding soy, ginger and mirin as a nod to our favorite Korean-style short ribs, galbi-jjim. Tangy, quick-pickled red cabbage makes a beautiful and zingy complement to the rich meat and savory sauce.

Preheat the oven to 325°F (165°C) and set a rack in the middle.

To cook the ribs, season the short ribs all over with the salt and pepper. Heat the oil in a large Dutch oven over medium-high heat. Working in batches so you don't crowd the pot, cook the ribs, turning them occasionally until they're well browned all over, 10 to 12 minutes per batch. Transfer them to a plate.

If there's a lot of fat in the pot, remove all but 2 tablespoons (30 ml), then add the onions, garlic and ginger. Cook, stirring often, until the onions are soft and translucent, 5 to 7 minutes. Add the wine, bring it to a boil and then reduce the heat and simmer until it reduces by half, 5 to 7 minutes. Add the mirin, soy sauce, maple syrup, fish sauce and star anise. Return the ribs to the pot, nestling them in as close to a single layer as possible, though some overlap is fine. Add enough water so the liquid comes almost to the top of the ribs, but doesn't cover them. Bring the liquid to a boil, cover the pot, place it in the oven and cook for 1½ hours, then nestle in the carrots and turnips. Continue to cook until the vegetables are tender and the meat is almost but not completely falling off the bone, 30 to 50 minutes.

Make the pickled red cabbage while the ribs are braising. In a bowl, toss together the cabbage, vinegar, sugar, salt and sesame oil, and let it stand at room temperature for at least 30 minutes, or transfer it to an airtight container and refrigerate for up to 4 days. Before serving, toss it with the scallions.

Transfer the ribs to a rimmed platter and set them aside. Remove the ginger and star anise pods and discard them. Use a spoon to skim as much fat off the top of the sauce as you can. If you want a thicker sauce, stir the cornstarch with 2 tablespoons (30 ml) of cold water in a small bowl until it dissolves. Stir the slurry into the braising liquid and simmer until the sauce thickens. Spoon the sauce and vegetables over the ribs. Serve them with pickled red cabbage and steamed rice. The short ribs can be made up to 3 days ahead of time and refrigerated in an airtight container. Reheat them in the Dutch oven over medium-low heat until hot. Add a little water if the sauce becomes too thick.

FOR THE RIBS

5 lbs (2.3 kg) English-cut, bone-in short ribs (4–5" [10–13 cm] long)

Kosher salt and freshly ground black pepper, as needed

2 tbsp (30 ml) neutral oil, plus more as needed

2 large yellow onions, halved and thinly sliced

1 large head garlic, cloves peeled and smashed

1 (3" [8-cm]) knob ginger, sliced into thin planks

2 cups (480 ml) dry red wine

½ cup (120 ml) mirin

½ cup (120 ml) soy sauce

¼ cup (60 ml) maple syrup

1 tbsp (15 ml) fish sauce

3 star anise pods

3 medium carrots, peeled and chopped

1 bunch Hakurei or baby turnips, trimmed and halved

2 tsp (5 g) cornstarch (optional)

FOR THE QUICK-PICKLED RED CABBAGE

6 cups (420 g) finely shredded red cabbage (about 1 medium head)

½ cup (120 ml) unseasoned rice vinegar

1 tbsp (13 g) sugar

1 tsp kosher salt

1 tbsp (15 ml) toasted sesame oil

4 scallions, finely sliced

FOR SERVING

Steamed rice

TACOS DE CARNITAS

Traditional carnitas are closer to a confit than a braise, where seasoned pork is simmered in lard until it becomes tender. We swap out the lard for a zesty mojo-style braising liquid perked up with loads of garlic and citrus. After the low-and-slow braise, the meat is shredded and crisped up in a skillet (or on a sheet tray under the broiler). This gives the dish a wonderful contrast of textures, with juicy, tender meat studded with crispy bits. (Everyone loves the crispy bits!) Once the carnitas are cooked, you can use them in a million different ways, but our favorite is tacos, with all the garnishes (and a few cold beers), please!

Preheat the oven to 275°F (135°C) and place a rack in the middle.

Cut the meat into 3-inch (8-cm) chunks, discarding any large pieces of fat. Add the cubes to the Dutch oven and toss with the salt, cumin, orange zest and juice, lime zest and juice and the garlic. Let the pork sit at room temperature for 30 minutes or refrigerate for up to 1 day. Add the onion, jalapeños, bay leaves, oregano, cinnamon, beer and maple syrup. Stir to combine, and add just enough water, if needed, to come up to the top layer of the pork. Turn the heat to high, bring the liquid to a boil and cover and place the pot in the oven. Cook until the pork is very tender when pierced with a fork, 2½ to 3 hours. Transfer the pork to a rimmed platter, let it cool slightly, then use two forks to shred it into bite-sized chunks. Remove the cinnamon stick and bay leaves from the liquid and discard. Use a spoon or a defatter to skim off some of the fat from the braising liquid. If you have a lot more than 2 cups (480 ml) of the liquid, turn the heat back on and boil until the liquid reduces down to about 2 cups (480 ml). Set the liquid aside.

You can crisp the shredded pork on a sheet tray under the broiler, but a skillet is the most effective method. Heat the oil in a large cast-iron or heavy skillet set over medium-high heat. Add about 2 cups (270 g) of pork to the pan and drizzle in 2 to 3 tablespoons (30 to 45 ml) of the reserved juices. Don't crowd the pan, and work in batches as necessary. Let the pork sear on one side, without moving it around, until some pieces turn crisp and brown, then toss it to warm up the other side. Add more liquid if needed to keep the pork moist.

To warm the tortillas, preheat a large skillet or grill pan over medium-high heat until hot. Working one tortilla at a time, dip a tortilla in a bowl filled with water. Place it on the hot skillet and cook until the tortilla is browned in spots, about 1 minute. Flip and cook for about 30 seconds longer. Transfer it to a tortilla warmer, or wrap it in a clean dish towel. Repeat with the remaining tortillas. To serve, add 2 to 3 tablespoons (15 to 30 g) of the carnitas mixture to the center of a tortilla (traditionally, 2 tortillas stacked on top of each other). Top with the garnishes, and serve with lime wedges.

4–5-lb (1.8–2.3-kg) boneless pork shoulder (also called Boston butt)

1 tbsp (8 g) kosher salt, plus more to taste

1 tbsp (6 g) ground cumin

2 medium oranges, zest finely grated, juiced

2 limes, zest finely grated, juiced

8 large cloves garlic, minced

1 large onion, diced

2 jalapeño peppers, deseeded and finely chopped

3 bay leaves

1½ tsp (2 g) dried oregano, preferably Mexican

1 cinnamon stick, broken in half

1 (12-oz [355-ml]) bottle lager-style beer

1 tbsp (15 ml) maple syrup

1 tbsp (15 ml) vegetable oil

24 small corn tortillas

FOR GARNISHING (OPTIONAL)

2 Hass avocados, sliced

1 bunch cilantro, leaves and tender stems, chopped

1 small white or red onion, finely chopped

10 small radishes, thinly sliced

2 jalapeño peppers, thinly sliced

Lime wedges

CRISPY PORK BELLY BRAISED IN SHERRY AND SOY

While most American pork tends to be lean, pork belly is the one cut where a rich layer of fat is gleefully indulged. The best pork belly dishes are a contrast in textures: soft, tender meat, topped with a cap of ultra-crisp, bubbly crackling. We like to braise it in a combination of soy, sherry wine and star anise, which adds a warm, almost nutty flavor. Pickled vegetables are a must, since their bright acidity cuts the richness of the pork fat. We love serving slices of the pork tucked into soft rolls, topped with big piles of pickles.

Preheat the oven to 250°F (120°C).

To prepare the pork, with a very sharp knife, score the pork skin in slits about ½ inch (1.3 cm) apart, cutting through the fat but not into the meat. Season the pork belly (both skin and flesh) all over with the salt, massaging it into the cuts. Rub the five-spice powder into the flesh—avoid getting it on the skin.

To prepare the braising liquid, add the soy sauce, dry sherry, vinegar, brown sugar, garlic, ginger and anise into a large Dutch oven and set it over medium heat. Bring it to a simmer and stir until the sugar dissolves. Gently lay in the pork, skin side up. (You can cut it in half if it doesn't fit as one piece.) Add enough water to bring the liquid three-quarters of the way to the top of the pork. Cover the pot and transfer it to the oven. Cook until the pork is very tender but not completely falling apart, 3 to 3½ hours.

While the pork is braising, make the pickles. Whisk the vinegar, sugar and salt in a small bowl until the sugar and salt dissolve. Add each vegetable to its own small bowl (so the colors don't bleed) and divide the brine between them. Let them sit, squeezing the vegetables gently with your hands occasionally to help them pickle more quickly. They'll be ready in about 10 minutes but can be made up to 3 days ahead of time. Cover and chill.

When the pork is tender, remove it from the oven and transfer it, skin side up, to a foil-lined rimmed baking sheet. Increase the oven temperature to 475°F (245°C). Roast the pork until the skin is puffed, brown and very crisp, 20 to 25 minutes.

Meanwhile, remove the ginger and star anise pods from the braising liquid and skim as much fat as you can from the top of the sauce. If you like a thicker sauce, add the cornstarch to a small bowl and stir in 1 tablespoon (15 ml) of cold water. Bring the liquid to a simmer and drizzle in the cornstarch slurry, stirring constantly, until the sauce thickens enough to coat the back of a spoon. Let the pork rest for at least 15 minutes before slicing. Serve it with the pickles, over rice or in buns, with the sauce available for drizzling.

FOR THE PORK

3–4-lb (1.4–1.8-kg) boneless, skin-on, center cut pork belly

1 tbsp (8 g) kosher salt

2 tbsp (12 g) Chinese five-spice powder

FOR THE BRAISING LIQUID

1 cup (240 ml) soy sauce

1 cup (240 ml) dry sherry or Shaoxing wine

2 tbsp (30 ml) unseasoned rice vinegar

6 tbsp (84 g) brown sugar

6 large cloves garlic, minced

1 (3" [8-cm]) knob fresh ginger, sliced into thin planks

2 star anise pods

2 tsp (5 g) cornstarch (optional)

FOR THE QUICK PICKLES

1 cup (240 ml) unseasoned rice vinegar

2 tbsp (26 g) sugar

2 tsp (6 g) kosher salt

4 cups (360 g) finely shredded or sliced vegetables (carrots, red cabbage, Persian cucumber, radishes)

FOR SERVING

Rice or buns

EASIER CHICKEN AND SAUSAGE CASSOULET

This rustic dish, a stew of velvety beans and tender, slow-cooked meat, is the pinnacle of French home cooking and can often take up to 4 days to prepare. Our version, made with chicken and two kinds of sausages, simplifies the process, but doesn't skimp on flavor.

To prepare the beans, the night before cooking, add the beans and 2 tablespoons (16 g) of salt to a large bowl, then add enough cold water to cover them by 4 inches (10 cm). Cover and let them sit overnight. The next day, drain the beans, add them to a large Dutch oven and cover with 2 inches (5 cm) of cold water. Add the onion, carrot, celery, garlic, pepper, bay leaf and 2 teaspoons (6 g) of the salt. Bring to a boil and simmer over medium heat, stirring occasionally, until the beans are cooked through, 1 to 1½ hours. Add the garlic sausage to the pot after 30 minutes. When the beans are cooked, remove and discard the onion, carrot and bay leaf. Drain the beans and sausage into a large, heatproof bowl and reserve the cooking liquid.

To cook the meat, preheat the oven to 350°F (180°C) and set a rack in the middle.

Return the Dutch oven to the stovetop over medium-high heat and add 2 tablespoons (30 ml) of the duck fat or olive oil. Season the chicken well with salt and pepper. Once the oil is shimmering, add the chicken thighs skin side down in a single layer. Cook, without disturbing, until the skin turns deep golden brown, 10 to 12 minutes. Turn and lightly brown the other side, 8 minutes. Remove the chicken to a plate and set it aside. Add the sausages and cook until well browned on all sides, about 15 minutes. Remove them to the plate with the chicken. If you like, cut the sausages in half on a steep angle.

Remove all but 2 to 3 tablespoons (30 to 45 ml) of the oil and add the diced onion, celery and carrots. Season lightly with salt and pepper, and cook until softened, about 10 minutes. Add 3 tablespoons (26 g) of the garlic (reserving 1 tablespoon [8 g]) and the tomato paste and cook until the garlic is fragrant and the paste turns a shade darker, 3 to 5 minutes. Add the rosemary, thyme, cloves, wine and tomatoes, and simmer for 5 minutes. Add the cooked beans and garlic sausage and stir to combine. Nestle the chicken thighs and Toulouse sausages into the beans, leaving some of the chicken partially exposed. Carefully pour some of the reserved bean liquid around the edges of the pot, until you can see liquid just at the top layer of the beans (but not covering them). You may not need to use all the liquid. If you don't have enough, use water or chicken stock.

Heat the remaining duck fat in a small skillet over medium heat. Add the remaining garlic and cook for 1 minute. Stir in the breadcrumbs, season with salt and pepper and cook, stirring, until they turn light golden brown, about 2 minutes. Spread the breadcrumb topping over the cassoulet and bake, uncovered, until bubbling and the crust is deep golden brown, about 1 hour. Serve in bowls all by itself: It needs no accompaniment.

FOR THE BEANS

1 lb (454 g) dried Tarbais, flageolet, Great Northern or cannellini beans

2 tbsp (16 g) plus 2 tsp (6 g) kosher salt, divided

Approximately 8 cups (2 L) cold water

1 small yellow onion, peeled and cut in half vertically

1 large carrot, peeled and cut in half

1 celery rib, cut in half

2 large cloves garlic, peeled and smashed

½ tsp freshly ground black pepper

1 bay leaf

8 oz (227 g) fully cooked French garlic sausage (*saucisson à l'ail*) or Polish kielbasa, skin removed and cut into 1" (2.5-cm) chunks

FOR THE MEAT

¼ cup (60 ml) duck fat or extra-virgin olive oil, divided, plus more as needed

6 bone-in, skin-on chicken thighs

Kosher salt and freshly ground black pepper, as needed

1 lb (454 g) Toulouse or other fresh pork sausage, pricked all over with a fork

1 large Spanish onion, diced

2 celery ribs, diced

2 large carrots, peeled and diced

8 large cloves garlic, finely chopped, divided (about ¼ cup [34 g])

2 tbsp (32 g) tomato paste

2 tsp (1 g) minced rosemary leaves

2 tsp (1 g) minced thyme

⅛ tsp ground cloves

1 cup (240 ml) dry white wine

1 (15-oz [425-g]) can crushed tomatoes

2 cups (100 g) coarse, fresh breadcrumbs or panko

SPICY KOREAN BRISKET SANDWICHES
WITH SESAME COLESLAW

Emily's two culinary influences are Jewish and Korean, and this recipe combines the two. Brisket, a staple of Jewish cuisine, is often braised with onions and tomatoes. We like to switch things up and use gochujang (spicy Korean chili paste), along with gochugaru (the chili powder used to make kimchi). They both have a rich, spicy flavor, transforming the braising liquid into a really excellent barbeque sauce. We like to serve it in toasted potato buns topped with a heap of crunchy homemade coleslaw.

If needed, cut the brisket into two or more pieces to fit into your Dutch oven. In a small bowl, mix together the salt, garlic powder, onion powder and gochugaru. Sprinkle the rub generously all over the meat, and press it in. You may not need all of it depending on the size of the brisket. Leave the brisket at room temperature for 1 hour, or cover it with plastic wrap and refrigerate for up to 24 hours.

Preheat the oven to 275°F (135°C) and place a rack in the lower middle slot.

To make the sauce, heat the oil in a large Dutch oven over medium-high heat. Add the onion, garlic and ginger and cook, stirring occasionally, until the onion turns soft and golden, 5 to 7 minutes. Add the wine, stock, gochujang, ketchup, soy sauce, brown sugar, Worcestershire sauce and fish sauce. Stir. Add the brisket to the Dutch oven. The liquid should be somewhere between one-half to three-quarters of the way up the meat. Add more stock or water, if needed. Bring the liquid to a boil. Cover the pot and transfer it to the oven. Cook, checking every hour and spooning braising liquid over the top, until the brisket is very tender, about 3½ hours. Remove the lid for the last hour of cooking. Transfer the beef to a plate or a rimmed cutting board and tent it with foil to keep it warm. Turn the heat to medium-low under the Dutch oven and simmer the sauce until it is reduced to about 3 cups (720 ml) (it will thicken more as it cools), 15 to 20 minutes. If you like a thicker sauce, stir in a cornstarch slurry: In a small bowl, stir together the cornstarch with 2 tablespoons (30 ml) of cold water. While the sauce is simmering, stir in half of the slurry. If the sauce still needs thickening, add the other half of the slurry.

FOR THE BRISKET

4–5-lb (1.8–2.3-kg) brisket (look for second cut, also called deckle), lightly trimmed of excess fat (see Note)

1½ tbsp (12 g) kosher salt, plus more to taste

1 tbsp (8 g) garlic powder

1 tbsp (7 g) onion powder

2 tbsp (14 g) gochugaru (Korean red chile powder) or 1 tbsp (7 g) hot paprika plus 1 tbsp (7 g) mild paprika

FOR THE SAUCE

2 tbsp (30 ml) neutral oil, plus more as needed

1 large Spanish onion, finely chopped (about 2 cups [320 g])

7 large cloves garlic, minced or grated (about 3 tbsp [25 g])

2 tbsp (12 g) grated fresh ginger

1 cup (240 ml) dry red wine

3 cups (720 ml) Golden Chicken Stock (page 84) or store-bought stock

¼ cup (64 g) gochujang (spicy Korean chili paste)

½ cup (120 ml) ketchup

2 tbsp (30 ml) soy sauce

3 tbsp (42 g) brown sugar

1 tbsp (15 ml) Worcestershire sauce

1 tbsp (15 ml) fish sauce

1 tbsp (8 g) cornstarch (optional)

(continued)

We like to make the brisket a full day (or up to 3 days) ahead. Place the unsliced brisket back in the Dutch oven and refrigerate overnight. Once it's cold, it's very easy to pull the solid fat off the top of the sauce. If you like thin, neat slices of brisket, take it out of the sauce and slice it, against the grain, while it's cold. To reheat it, place the slices back in the pot with sauce, bring it to a simmer over low and heat until it's warmed through. You can also heat the pot in a 275°F (135°C) oven until hot, about 15 minutes.

If you're serving it the same day, let the brisket rest for at least 20 minutes before slicing. Make sure to use a sharp knife and cut against the grain. (If you look at the brisket, you'll see the muscle fibers running in one direction. Cutting across these fibers shortens them, which makes for a tender piece of meat. If you slice with the grain, the brisket will be stringy and difficult to chew, no matter how you've cooked it.) Use a fat separator or a spoon to skim the fat off the sauce.

To make the coleslaw, add the cabbages to a large bowl and toss with the salt. In a small bowl, mix together the sesame oil, rice vinegar and mayonnaise. Add the dressing to the cabbage along with the scallions and sesame seeds and toss to combine. To serve, pile some brisket onto a bun, drizzle over some of the sauce and top it with coleslaw and some cucumbers, if desired. Have plenty of napkins handy.

NOTE: The first cut, also known as the flat cut, or center cut, is lean and may dry out during cooking. The second cut, or deckle, is fattier and thus has more flavor. Trim any large, thick pieces of fat, but leave a fat cap, which will baste the meat as it braises.

FOR THE COLESLAW

3 cups (210 g) finely shredded napa cabbage

2 cups (140 g) finely shredded red cabbage

1 tsp kosher salt

1 tbsp (15 ml) toasted sesame oil

2 tbsp (30 ml) unseasoned rice vinegar

¼ cup (60 ml) mayonnaise (preferably Japanese-style)

3 scallions, finely sliced

2 tbsp (18 g) toasted sesame seeds (preferably a mix of black and white)

FOR SERVING

Potato buns or sandwich rolls

3 small Persian cucumbers, thinly sliced (optional)

CRISPY BRAISED DUCK LEGS
WITH LENTILS

When we really want to impress our dinner guests, we make duck. We once had duck legs in France that were so delicious that we diverted our road trip just to go back to the same restaurant the following week and eat them again. Duck skin is extremely fatty, but its meat is very lean and can be tough, so the best way to prepare it is low and slow so that the legs slowly braise, or confit, in their own rendered fat, making them gorgeously tender. They finish cooking over French lentils, which are brightened up with a bracing splash of sherry vinegar.

FOR THE DUCK

4–6 duck legs (4–5 lbs [1.8–2.3 kg])

2 tsp (6 g) kosher salt

1 tsp freshly ground black pepper

1 tsp crushed fennel seed

To make the duck, dry the duck legs well with paper towels. In a small bowl, mix together the salt, pepper and fennel seed. Lay the duck legs onto a rimmed baking sheet and rub the mixture all over them, lightly pressing it into the skin and meat. Place the legs in the refrigerator, skin side up, uncovered, for at least 2 hours (or up to 48 hours) to let the skin dry.

When you're ready to cook, preheat the oven to 225°F (110°C) and set a rack in the middle.

Heat a large Dutch oven over medium heat, and add the duck legs in a single layer, skin side down (no need to add any oil). Cook them in batches if they don't fit easily in a single layer. Press them down to make sure there is good contact between the skin and the pan. Cook until the skin is a deep golden brown, 8 to 10 minutes. Turn the legs over and brown the other side, 5 minutes. If you've cooked the legs in batches, transfer all the legs and any accumulated juices back to the pot, skin side down, nestling them in as close to a single layer as you can get. There will be a lot of fat in the pot, and that's what you want. Cover the pot, transfer to the oven and cook for 2½ hours. Remove the pot from the oven and transfer the legs to a large plate or sheet pan. Increase the temperature of the oven to 400°F (200°C).

Carefully remove all but 2 tablespoons (30 ml) of the duck fat from the pot and into a heatproof bowl (a turkey baster works well for this) and reserve the fat for another use (you can freeze it for long-term storage [see Note]).

(continued)

For the lentils, place the pot back on the stovetop and set the heat to medium. Add the carrots, onions and fennel, along with a good pinch of salt and pepper, and cook, stirring occasionally, until the vegetables begin to soften but not brown, about 7 minutes. Add the garlic, thyme, rosemary and bay leaf and cook for 1 minute. Add the lentils, stock and potato. Cook uncovered, stirring occasionally, until the lentils are tender, 20 to 25 minutes. If the lentils become dry before they are tender, add a little more stock or water to keep them mostly submerged.

Place the duck legs on top of the lentils, skin side up, in a single layer (they will have shrunk substantially by this point). Return the pot to the oven, uncovered, and cook until the duck legs are crispy, 10 to 15 minutes. Remove the pot from the oven and transfer the duck legs to a plate. Remove the bay leaf from the lentils and stir in the spinach until it wilts. Stir in 2 tablespoons (30 ml) of vinegar, and season to taste with the rest of the vinegar, salt and pepper. To serve, spoon the lentils onto plates, swirl in a little crème fraîche or sour cream, if using, and top with the crispy duck legs. Garnish with the reserved fennel fronds.

NOTE: The duck fat you'll have left over is worth its weight in gold. Use it for recipes such as Brazilian-Style Collard Greens (page 54) or for roasting potatoes.

FOR THE LENTILS

2 carrots, peeled and finely chopped

2 medium yellow onions, peeled and finely chopped

1 large fennel bulb, finely chopped, fronds reserved for garnish

Kosher salt and freshly ground black pepper, as needed

5 medium cloves garlic, minced

2 tsp (1 g) minced fresh thyme

2 tsp (1 g) minced fresh rosemary

1 bay leaf

2½ cups (454 g) Puy lentils

5½ cups (1.3 L) low-sodium chicken or vegetable stock

1 medium russet potato, peeled and roughly chopped

1 small bunch baby spinach (about 6–8 oz [170–227 g])

4 tbsp (60 ml) sherry vinegar, divided

Crème fraîche or sour cream (optional)

OSSO BUCO

When many people hear the term braising, they think of osso buco. To us, it's the ultimate date night or dinner party dish, and serving it essentially says, "I really, really like you"—and not just because the name literally translates to, "bone with a hole." The dish's moniker refers to the hole in the center of a crosscut veal shank, wherein hides the prized delicacy: rich, buttery bone marrow.

Preheat the oven to 325°F (165°C) and set a rack in the middle.

To prepare the meat and veggies, season the veal shanks generously with salt and pepper. If you want your braised shanks to remain perfectly round, tie a length of butcher's twine tightly around the meaty circumference of each piece. Add the flour to a shallow bowl. Lightly dredge each shank all over in flour, shaking off any excess. Heat the olive oil in a large Dutch oven set over medium-high heat. When the oil is shimmering, add the shanks to the pot, working in batches if necessary, in order to not overcrowd the pot. Cook the shanks, turning occasionally, until the meat is well browned on both sides, about 5 minutes per side. Adjust the heat as needed to avoid burning the flour. Remove the browned shanks to a platter and repeat with the remaining shanks, adding more oil to the pot if needed. Set the browned shanks aside.

Remove the oil from the pot, turn the heat down to medium and add the butter. When the butter is melted, add the onions, carrots, celery and garlic, along with a pinch of salt. Cook, stirring often, until the vegetables are softened and turn a light golden color, about 7 minutes. Add the wine and cook, scraping up any brown bits with a wooden spoon, until the wine is reduced to about ½ cup (120 ml), about 3 minutes. Add the tomato paste and cook, stirring often, until it turns a dark brick-red, about 2 minutes. Stir in the stock, diced tomatoes, bay leaves, rosemary and thyme. Add back the veal shanks, along with any accumulated juices, arranging them in an even layer, though a little overlap is okay. The liquid should come about three-quarters of the way to the top of the shanks. If it doesn't, add more stock or water as needed. Bring the liquid to a simmer, cover the pot, place it in the oven and cook until the meat is very tender, almost falling off the bone, 1½ to 2 hours.

When the shanks are almost done cooking, make the gremolata. In a small bowl, stir together the parsley, lemon zest, garlic and anchovies. Set aside.

Carefully transfer the cooked shanks to a platter, using a wide spatula and tongs to keep them from falling apart. Cover the platter with foil and set it aside. Use a spoon to skim off any excess fat on the surface of the sauce and add 2 tablespoons (30 g) of the gremolata to the sauce. The liquid should be nice and thick, but you can adjust the consistency by either adding a little stock or simmering it on the stovetop to reduce it. Discard the bay leaves, rosemary and thyme, and season the sauce with salt and pepper, if necessary.

Remove any twine from the shanks, and spoon the braising sauce on top of the meat. Serve the remaining gremolata on the side, and use small spoons or knives for scooping out the marrow from the bones. Osso buco is traditionally served with saffron-infused risotto, but we like it with simple buttery polenta.

FOR THE MEAT AND VEGGIES

4–6 small veal or pork shanks (about 4 lbs [1.8 kg])

Kosher salt and freshly ground black pepper, as needed

1 cup (125 g) all-purpose flour

2 tbsp (30 ml) extra-virgin olive oil, plus more if needed

4 tbsp (56 g) unsalted butter

2 large yellow onions, finely diced

2 medium carrots, finely diced

2 medium celery ribs, finely diced

4 medium cloves garlic, minced

1½ cups (360 ml) dry white wine

2 tbsp (32 g) tomato paste

¾ cup (180 ml) Golden Chicken Stock (page 84) or store-bought stock

1 (28-oz [794-g]) can diced tomatoes

2 bay leaves

1 (5" [13-cm]) rosemary sprig

4 thyme sprigs

FOR THE GREMOLATA

3 tbsp (12 g) finely minced flat-leaf parsley leaves and tender stems

Zest of 1 large lemon

3 medium cloves garlic, finely grated or minced

2 anchovy fillets, minced

FOR SERVING

Polenta or saffron-infused risotto

CHICKEN BRAISED IN MILK

In culinary terms, the word broken usually indicates a problem. A vinaigrette that won't emulsify, a hollandaise split with blobs of butter. But in this recipe, originally popularized by chef and restauranteur Jamie Oliver, the breaking of the sauce is not just on purpose, but a revelation. The acidity in the lemon peel breaks the milk into curds, which also happens to be the first step in making cheese, like ricotta. The resulting sauce—garlicky and fragrant with woodsy herbs like rosemary and sage—is addictive.

1 (3–4-lb [1.4–1.8-kg]) whole chicken

Kosher salt and freshly ground black pepper, as needed

¼ cup (60 ml) melted unsalted butter or extra-virgin olive oil (or a mix)

1 large head of garlic, root trimmed, outer skin removed and cut in half horizontally

3 medium shallots, chopped (about 1 cup [160 g])

5 fresh sage leaves

3 large fresh rosemary sprigs

Zest of 2 lemons, peeled in thick strips with a vegetable peeler

¼ tsp freshly grated nutmeg

2½ cups (600 ml) whole milk

Boiled potatoes, green salad or roasted vegetables, for serving

Dry the chicken well and season it very generously all over with salt and pepper, including inside the cavity. If you have time, do this several hours ahead or even the day before you plan to cook, and refrigerate it, uncovered, until you're ready. Remove it from the refrigerator 30 minutes before you plan to cook it.

Heat the oven to 375°F (190°C) and set a rack in the middle.

Set a medium Dutch oven (ideally one that will fit the chicken snugly, without too much extra room) over medium-high heat, and add the butter or olive oil. When the fat is hot, add the chicken to the pot and sear it, turning it every few minutes until the skin has turned crisp and deep golden brown all over, about 10 minutes. Turn the heat down to low, remove the chicken from the pot and set it on a plate. Remove all but 2 to 3 tablespoons (30 to 45 ml) of the fat from the pot. Add the garlic, cut side down, and the shallots, and cook, stirring occasionally, until the shallots begin to soften, about 3 minutes. Return the chicken to the pot, breast side up, and scatter in the sage, rosemary, lemon zest and nutmeg. Pour in the milk, bring it to a simmer and then place the pot in the oven and cook, basting the chicken occasionally, until the chicken is cooked through (165°F [75°C] on an instant-read thermometer) and the liquid has reduced to a thick, broken sauce, about 1½ hours. If the sauce reduces too quickly, place the lid partway over the pot and continue cooking.

When the chicken is ready, remove it to a platter and cover it loosely with foil. Using tongs, squeeze the garlic halves, so the soft cloves fall into the sauce. Taste the sauce for seasoning, adding salt and pepper, as desired, and spoon the sauce over the chicken. Serve it with boiled potatoes and a green salad or roasted vegetables.

SLOW-BRAISED LAMB SHOULDER AND POTATOES
WITH YOGURT-MINT SAUCE

For reasons we have yet to understand, many Americans' only experience with lamb is with tiny, pink-in-the-center rib chops: delicious, but prohibitively expensive and difficult to cook for a crowd. But a shoulder roast, cooked low and slow in wine, garlic, fennel and rosemary, is a different kind of beast. It becomes so tender you barely even need a knife to cut it. Throw away that jar of mint jelly: The fresh yogurt-mint sauce we serve this with will make a convert out of you.

The day before you plan to cook the lamb, use a sharp paring knife to make small slits all over the lamb about 2 inches (5 cm) apart. Add the garlic, salt, pepper, lemon zest, rosemary and ¼ cup (60 ml) of the olive oil to the bowl of a food processor. Pulse until a coarse paste forms, 10 to 15 one-second pulses. Rub the paste all over the lamb, pressing it into the slits. Place the lamb on a rimmed baking sheet or a plate, cover it with plastic wrap and refrigerate for 12 to 24 hours. Remove the lamb from the refrigerator about 1 hour before you plan to cook.

Preheat the oven to 300°F (150°C) and set a rack in the lower third.

Heat the remaining olive oil in a large Dutch oven set over medium-high heat. Add the onion and fennel, season with a pinch of salt and pepper and cook, stirring often, until the vegetables begin to soften, 7 to 10 minutes. Place the lamb in the pot and pour the wine and stock around it. Cover the pot, place it in the oven and cook until the lamb is tender but not falling apart, about 2½ hours.

While the lamb is braising, make the yogurt-mint sauce. In a small bowl, stir together the yogurt, garlic, mint, lemon juice and reserved fennel fronds. Season with salt and pepper to taste and set it aside. The sauce can be made up to 1 day ahead and refrigerated.

Increase the oven temperature to 450°F (230°C).

Add the potatoes around the lamb, spoon the pomegranate molasses over the top of the lamb, return the pot to the oven and cook, uncovered, until the potatoes are tender and the top of the lamb is browned. This will take 45 minutes to 1 hour. During this time, carefully baste the lamb every 15 minutes with the accumulated juices, using a spoon or baster. Carefully transfer the lamb and potatoes to a platter, loosely cover with foil and let it rest for 10 minutes. Skim any excess fat off the braising liquid, and serve it with the lamb, along with the yogurt-mint sauce. The meat will be too tender to slice neatly, so use a fork to pull it apart.

FOR THE LAMB AND POTATOES

4–5-lb (1.8–2.3-kg) bone-in lamb shoulder roast, tied

12 cloves garlic, peeled

1½ tbsp (12 g) kosher salt, plus more to taste

1 tsp freshly ground black pepper, plus more to taste

Zest from 1 lemon

4 sprigs fresh rosemary

¼ cup (60 ml) plus 2 tbsp (30 ml) extra-virgin olive oil, divided

1 large onion, chopped

1 large fennel bulb, chopped, fronds chopped and reserved for the sauce

1½ cups (360 ml) dry white wine

1 cup (240 ml) Golden Chicken Stock (page 84) or store-bought stock

2 lbs (908 g) baby Yukon Gold potatoes

2 tbsp (30 ml) pomegranate molasses (store-bought or see homemade technique in Moroccan-Spiced Eggplant and Chickpeas on page 44)

FOR THE YOGURT-MINT SAUCE

1 cup (240 ml) Greek yogurt

1 small clove garlic, minced or grated

3 tbsp (18 g) finely chopped mint leaves

1 tbsp (15 ml) lemon juice

Kosher salt and freshly ground black pepper, to taste

CHICKEN, SHALLOTS AND PEAS BRAISED IN WHITE BALSAMIC VINEGAR

White balsamic vinegar is the lighter, fruitier version of the more common dark balsamic that you probably have lurking at the back of your pantry. We use this golden-hued vinegar to form the base of an agrodolce (sweet and sour) sauce that coats this simple dish of sautéed chicken, shallots and peas. Frozen peas are one of the few vegetables that are often as good as fresh—and we love them unapologetically—but if fresh spring pea shoots are available, a bright shower of them makes a colorful, delicious topping.

Generously season both sides of the chicken pieces with salt and pepper. Add the flour to a wide, shallow bowl and dredge each piece of chicken until it's thoroughly coated, shaking off any excess flour. Place a large Dutch oven over medium-high heat and add the oil. When the oil is shimmering, add the chicken in a single layer, working in batches as needed. Cook until light golden brown, about 4 minutes, then flip and cook for 4 minutes on the other side. Remove the chicken to a plate and repeat with the other pieces, if necessary, adding a little more oil if the pan looks dry.

When all the chicken is browned, turn the heat down to medium and add the shallots, again adding a little oil if the pan is dry. Cook, stirring occasionally, until the shallots begin to soften, about 4 minutes. Add the garlic and cook, until fragrant, about 30 seconds. Pour in the vinegar and wine and scrape the bottom of the pan with a wooden spoon to loosen any brown bits. Simmer until the liquid reduces by half, about 10 minutes, then stir in the chicken stock and honey. Bring the liquid to a boil, and then lower the heat to a bare simmer and add the chicken pieces back to the pot, along with any accumulated juices. Cover and cook until the chicken is cooked through (165°F [75°C] on an instant-read thermometer) and the shallots are tender, about 15 minutes for breasts or 20 minutes for thighs. Stir in the peas after 10 minutes.

Transfer the chicken to a platter and cover it loosely with foil. With the heat still on low, whisk the butter into the sauce, stirring constantly. Check for seasoning and add salt and pepper to taste. Spoon the shallots, peas and sauce over the chicken and garnish with the pine nuts and pea shoots, if you're using them. Serve with baby potatoes or egg noodles.

2½–3 lbs (1.1–1.4 kg) boneless, skinless chicken thighs or breasts

Kosher salt and freshly ground black pepper, as needed

¾ cup (94 g) all-purpose flour

2 tbsp (30 ml) extra-virgin olive oil, plus more as needed

10 medium shallots, peeled, root trimmed and cut in half vertically

3 medium cloves garlic, minced

¾ cup (180 ml) white balsamic vinegar

½ cup (120 ml) dry white wine or vermouth

1 cup (240 ml) Golden Chicken Stock (page 84) or store-bought stock

1 tbsp (15 ml) honey

1 (12-oz [340-g]) bag frozen baby peas

2 tbsp (28 g) cold unsalted butter

¼ cup (35 g) toasted pine nuts (optional)

¼ cup (5 g) fresh pea shoots (optional)

Baby potatoes or egg noodles, for serving

CHICKEN ADOBO

Adobo is Spanish for marinade, and Filipino adobo specifically refers to a method of marinating and braising a protein (usually, but not exclusively, chicken) in a piquant mixture of vinegar, soy sauce and spices. It's an inexpensive rustic dish that quickly becomes an obsession. We like to keep it simple, with garlic, bay leaf, black pepper and just a little sugar for balance. A great aspect of the dish is that the flavorings are multipurpose, acting as a marinade, braising liquid and finally, a glaze.

In a large, nonreactive bowl, stir together the garlic, jalapeño, vinegar, soy sauce, bay leaves, sugar and pepper. Add the chicken and move it around to coat every piece. Cover the bowl with plastic wrap and marinate the chicken at room temperature for 30 minutes, or refrigerate for up to 24 hours.

Preheat the oven to 325°F (165°C) and place a rack in the middle.

Remove the chicken from the marinade and pat the pieces dry with paper towels. Reserve the marinade. Heat a large Dutch oven over medium-high heat and add the oil. When the oil is shimmering, add the chicken, skin side down, working in batches if necessary. Cook, without disturbing, until the skin is a deep golden brown, 10 to 12 minutes. Transfer the chicken to a plate and remove any fat from the pot. Pour in the reserved marinade along with the water. Nestle the chicken thighs into the pot, skin side up, and bring the liquid to a boil. Cover the pot, transfer it to the oven and cook until the chicken is cooked through and tender, but not falling off the bone, about 45 minutes.

Return the pot to the stovetop and remove the lid. Set the heat to medium-high and simmer the braising liquid, occasionally turning the chicken in the sauce, until the liquid has thickened enough to coat the chicken thighs, 5 to 7 minutes. Remove and discard the bay leaves. Serve the chicken over steamed rice with extra sauce spooned over the top. Garnish with scallions and a few slices of jalapeño, if desired.

1 head garlic, cloves peeled and smashed

1 jalapeño pepper, sliced (seeds discarded if desired), plus more for garnish

1 cup (240 ml) unseasoned coconut, palm or rice vinegar

1 cup (240 ml) soy sauce

4 bay leaves

1 tbsp (14 g) palm or brown sugar

2 tsp (4 g) freshly ground black pepper

8 bone-in, skin-on chicken thighs (about 3 lbs [1.4 kg])

1 tbsp (15 ml) vegetable oil

½ cup (120 ml) water

Steamed rice, for serving

2 scallions, thinly sliced

SPICED LAMB SHANK TAGINE

You don't need a traditional tagine, the cone-shaped earthenware pot typically from North Africa, to make this tender, fragrant, spiced braised lamb. A Dutch oven does essentially the same thing, trapping and circulating aromatic condensation as the lamb cooks, which helps to keep the stew moist. This dish looks like a party and tastes just as good: a traditional mix of cinnamon and other spices; sweet, melting apricots; and an explosion of freshness from the mint and pomegranate garnishes.
This is a dinner party slam dunk.

Trim the shanks of excess fat, then season them generously with salt and pepper. In a small bowl, stir together the garlic, ginger, paprika, sumac, Aleppo pepper, cumin, turmeric and cardamom, and coat the shanks all over with the paste. Leave the shanks at room temperature for at least 1 hour, or cover with plastic wrap and refrigerate them overnight; return to room temperature before proceeding.

Preheat the oven to 350°F (180°C) and set a rack in the middle.

Melt the butter in a large (preferably oval) Dutch oven set over medium-high heat. Add the onions and the cinnamon sticks and sprinkle them with salt. Cook, stirring often, until the onions begin to soften, about 5 minutes. Stir in the tomato paste and cook until the paste turns a shade darker, about 3 minutes. Add the shanks and cook, moving them around and turning them occasionally, until they are lightly browned in spots, about 10 minutes. If the onions begin to darken too much, lower the heat to medium and stir in 1 to 2 tablespoons (15 to 30 ml) of water.

Pour in the chicken stock, sugar and apricots. Add enough water so the liquid just barely covers the shanks. Bring to a simmer, cover the pot and place it in the oven. Cook until the meat is very tender and almost falling from the bone, 2 to 2½ hours. Carefully transfer the meat to a serving platter. Use a spoon to skim off some of the fat from the surface of the cooking liquid, stir in the pomegranate molasses and simmer for a few minutes to reduce the sauce slightly. Taste for seasoning, and then pour the sauce over the meat. Serve with couscous, and garnish the platter with pomegranate seeds, slivered red onion and plenty of mint.

The tagine may be prepared up to 2 days ahead of time. Reheat gently in a covered pot on the stovetop, adding a little more water as necessary.

6 small or 4 large lamb shanks (about 5 lbs [2.3 kg])

Kosher salt and freshly ground black pepper, as needed

7 large cloves garlic, minced or grated

2 tbsp (12 g) grated fresh ginger

1 tbsp (7 g) paprika

1 tbsp (8 g) ground sumac

2 tsp (4 g) Aleppo-style pepper or 1 tsp crushed red pepper flakes

2 tsp (4 g) ground cumin

1½ tsp (3 g) ground turmeric

½ tsp ground cardamom

2 tbsp (28 g) unsalted butter or 2 tbsp (30 ml) extra-virgin olive oil

3 cups (480 g) chopped yellow onions (about 2 large onions)

2 (4" [10-cm]) cinnamon sticks

2 tbsp (32 g) tomato paste

2 cups (480 ml) Golden Chicken Stock (page 84) or store-bought stock

1 tbsp (14 g) lightly packed brown sugar

6 oz (170 g) dried apricots, roughly chopped (about 25–30 apricots)

1 tbsp (15 ml) pomegranate molasses (store-bought or see homemade technique in Moroccan-Spiced Eggplant and Chickpeas on page 44)

Couscous, for serving

Pomegranate seeds, for garnish

½ small red onion, very thinly sliced, for garnish

1 bunch mint, for garnish

CHICKEN PAPRIKASH
WITH BUTTERED EGG NOODLES

Emily's introduction to this dish was unconventional: Her good friend Rebecca grew up in the Squat Theatre, the Hungarian experimental theater company. Their Manhattan building was often bustling with New York City artists, many of them Hungarian, and this dish of chicken braised in gravy rich with paprika was a staple. And since this recipe description is already rife with arcane and random information, let's continue: What dish did Jonathan Harker eat on his way to Dracula's castle in Bram Stoker's 1897 novel? If you said "Chicken Paprikash," you win a bite on the neck.

3–4-lb (1.4–1.8-kg) bone-in, skin-on chicken, cut into 6 pieces (or 4 large chicken thighs)

Kosher salt and freshly ground black pepper, as needed

3 tbsp (42 g) unsalted butter, divided

1 large Spanish onion, diced

5 medium cloves garlic, minced

3 tbsp (24 g) all-purpose flour

3 tbsp (21 g) sweet Hungarian paprika

2 cups (480 ml) Golden Chicken Stock (page 84) or store-bought stock

1 (15-oz [425-g]) can crushed tomatoes

½ cup (120 ml) dry white wine

1 (12-oz [340-g]) bag wide egg noodles

¼ cup (15 g) roughly chopped parsley leaves, divided

½ cup (120 ml) sour cream, room temperature, plus more for serving

Aleppo-style pepper, for garnish (optional)

Preheat the oven to 325°F (165°C) and set a rack in the middle.

Dry the chicken well and season it all over with salt and pepper. Melt 2 tablespoons (30 g) of the butter in a large Dutch oven over medium-high heat. Add the chicken, skin side down, in batches if necessary, and cook until the skin is golden brown and crisp, 8 to 10 minutes. Transfer the chicken to a plate and set it aside.

If there's a lot of fat in the pot, pour off all but 2 tablespoons (30 ml) and reduce the heat to medium. Add the onion and garlic, along with a good pinch of salt and pepper. Cook, stirring and scraping the browned bits on the bottom of the pot with a wooden spoon until the onion is soft and light brown, 5 to 7 minutes. Stir in the flour and cook for 2 minutes. Add the paprika and stir just until it coats the onion, about 1 minute. Add the chicken stock, tomatoes and wine. Nestle the chicken back into the pot, skin side up, along with any accumulated juices. Bring the liquid to a boil, cover the pot and transfer it to the oven. Cook until the chicken is very tender, 40 to 45 minutes.

While the chicken is cooking, bring a large pot of salted water to a boil. Add the egg noodles and cook according to the package instructions. Drain the noodles well and tip them back into the hot pot. Add the remaining butter and half of the parsley, and toss until the butter is melted and the noodles are coated. Season with salt and pepper to taste.

Once the chicken is cooked, transfer it to a plate and set it aside. Spoon about ½ cup (120 ml) of the sauce into a small bowl and stir in the sour cream until combined. (This raises the temperature of the sour cream so it doesn't separate when mixed with the hot sauce.) Pour the sour cream mix back into the pot and stir to combine. Season the sauce with salt and pepper to taste, return the chicken to the sauce and simmer it for a few minutes to heat through. Serve over the buttered egg noodles, garnished with the rest of the parsley and a sprinkling of Aleppo-style pepper, if using.

HARD CIDER-BRAISED TURKEY THIGHS
WITH APPLES AND ONIONS

A few years ago, our Thanksgiving plans fell through and we decided to have a scaled-down feast for two (plus plenty of leftovers, of course). We wanted all the flavors of Turkey Day without having to roast an entire turkey. Dutch oven to the rescue! Braising the turkey thighs in a dry hard cider makes them incredibly moist and tender, and creates a delicious apple and onion gravy. We love hard cider for drinking, and its crisp, citrusy flavor goes particularly well with turkey, both in and out of the pot.

4 bone-in, skin-on turkey thighs or 2 thighs and 2 legs (about 4 lbs [1.8 kg])

Kosher salt and freshly ground black pepper, as needed

2 tbsp (30 ml) vegetable oil

4 large yellow onions, halved, thinly sliced pole to pole (about 4 cups [640 g])

4 celery ribs, diced

3 medium carrots, peeled and diced

8 large cloves garlic, finely chopped

2 (12-oz [355-ml]) bottles hard apple cider (preferably a dry, English-style variety; see Note)

2 tsp (2 g) minced fresh thyme leaves

10 small sage leaves, minced

2 cups (480 ml) Golden Chicken Stock (page 84) or store-bought stock

3 apples (Granny Smith, Honeycrisp or Braeburn recommended), peeled, cored and cut into thick wedges

2 tbsp (28 g) room temperature unsalted butter

2 tbsp (16 g) all-purpose flour

½ tbsp (8 ml) Dijon mustard

Preheat the oven to 325°F (165°C) and set a rack in the middle.

Dry the turkey thighs well and season them very generously with salt and pepper. If you have the time, do this 1 to 2 days ahead and refrigerate, uncovered, to allow the turkey to absorb the seasoning. Remove them from the refrigerator at least 30 minutes before cooking.

Heat the oil in a large Dutch oven, set over medium-high heat. When the oil is shimmering, add the thighs skin side down, making sure not to crowd the pot; cook them in batches as necessary. Cook on one side, without disturbing, until the skin turns deep brown, about 10 minutes. Turn and sear the other side for 5 minutes and transfer them to a large plate. Repeat with the remaining thighs. If you're using legs, turn them every few minutes so they brown on all sides.

Add the onions, celery and carrots, season with salt and pepper, and cook, stirring often, until the onions turn soft and light brown, about 15 minutes. Add the garlic and cook for 1 minute. Add the cider, thyme and sage, scraping up any brown bits with a wooden spoon. Bring to a boil, reduce the heat and simmer until the liquid is reduced by half, about 8 minutes. Add the stock and nestle in the turkey, skin side up. Bring to a boil, cover the pot, place it in the oven and cook for 2 hours. Add the apples to the pot and cook, uncovered, until the apples are soft and the meat is almost falling off the bone, about 1 hour longer. Meanwhile, mix together the butter and flour in a small bowl until a uniform paste (a beurre manié) is formed, and set aside.

Return the pot to the stovetop, remove the turkey and apples to a serving platter and cover loosely with foil. Turn the heat to medium and bring the liquid to a simmer. Whisk in the beurre manié a little at a time until the sauce is thickened to your liking. Stir in the mustard, taste for seasoning and spoon the hot gravy over the turkey and apples.

NOTE: We used a combination from two of our favorite local cideries, Angry Orchard's Stone Dry and Treasury Cider's Wiccopee.

RED WINE-BRAISED SHALLOTS AND RADICCHIO

Radicchio is a gorgeous magenta vegetable that looks like a lettuce or cabbage but is actually in the chicory family. While we love its bitter flavor in salads (especially when paired with honey and good blue cheese), braising mellows its bite and brings out some of its essential sweetness. Shallots make a great companion, turning caramelized and silky in the sweet-and-sour wine-based braise. This makes a great side to serve with any kind of roast, but it's equally happy as a first course when paired with something rich and fatty, like chicken liver pâté.

4 oz (113 g) pancetta, cut into small cubes

10 shallots, peeled, cut vertically through the root end

1 tbsp (15 ml) extra-virgin olive oil, if needed

3 medium heads radicchio, each cut through the core into 4 wedges

Kosher salt and freshly ground black pepper, as needed

2 sprigs rosemary

1 cup (240 ml) Golden Chicken Stock (page 84) or store-bought stock

½ cup (120 ml) dry red wine

1 tbsp (15 ml) balsamic vinegar

2½ tbsp (35 g) packed light brown sugar

1 tbsp (14 g) unsalted butter

Add the pancetta to a large Dutch oven set over medium heat. Cook, stirring occasionally, until the pancetta is brown and crisp and most of the fat is rendered. Use a slotted spoon to remove the cubes to a paper towel–lined plate, leaving the fat in the pot. Add the shallots and cook, stirring occasionally, until they soften and turn light brown in spots, 5 to 7 minutes. Remove the shallots to a plate and set them aside. If the pot is dry, add a tablespoon (15 ml) of olive oil. Turn the heat up to high and add the radicchio, nestling it into the pot as best you can, or working in batches if needed. Season with salt and pepper, and let them sear until they brown on the bottom, about 2 minutes, and then turn and brown the other side, 2 minutes.

Return the shallots to the pot and stir in the rosemary, chicken stock, wine, balsamic vinegar and brown sugar. Bring to a boil over high heat, then reduce it to a simmer and cook, uncovered, turning occasionally, until the shallots are completely tender and the radicchio is wilted, 5 to 7 minutes. Remove the radicchio and shallots to a platter and discard the rosemary. Turn the heat back up and boil the liquid until it reduces by a third, about 3 minutes. Turn the heat off and whisk the butter into the pot until it melts and the sauce thickens, and season to taste with salt and pepper. Pour the glaze over the vegetables, sprinkle over the reserved pancetta and serve hot or at room temperature.

NOTE: For a vegetarian version, skip the pancetta and cook the vegetables in 2 tablespoons (30 ml) of olive oil.

Yield: 4 servings

MOROCCAN-SPICED EGGPLANT AND CHICKPEAS

In high school, Emily waitressed at a Middle Eastern restaurant and jazz bar on the Upper West Side of Manhattan. She was a terrible waitress, mostly because she spent more time in the kitchen bribing the cooks to give up their recipe secrets than serving customers. One of her favorite stolen recipes was for imam bayildi *(whole eggplant stuffed with onion, garlic and tomatoes and simmered in olive oil). We've taken the flavors from that dish, added chickpeas to make it more of a meal and cooked it like a stew. Layering the ingredients helps keep the eggplant slices from falling apart, and they become extra silky and luscious. Don't skimp on the mint, as it's key to the bright flavor.*

To make homemade pomegranate molasses, add the pomegranate juice, sugar and lemon juice to a 4-quart (4-L) saucepan set over medium heat. Cook, stirring occasionally, until the sugar has completely dissolved. Reduce the heat to medium-low and gently simmer until the mixture has reduced to about 1 cup (240 ml), 60 to 75 minutes. It should be the consistency of thick maple syrup. Remove the pan from the heat and set it aside to cool for 30 minutes. Transfer the molasses to a clean glass jar and allow it to cool completely before covering and storing it in the refrigerator for up to 6 months.

To make the eggplant, partially peel the eggplants in strips down the length of the fruits, leaving alternating strips of peel so that they appear striped. This will help them retain their shape while cooking. Cut each eggplant in half lengthwise, then slice them into 1-inch (2.5-cm)-thick half-moons. Set them on a rimmed baking sheet and sprinkle them generously with salt. Let them stand for 1 hour. Rinse the eggplants and pat them dry.

Preheat the oven to 375°F (190°C) and set a rack in the middle.

Heat 2 tablespoons (30 ml) of the olive oil in a large Dutch oven set over medium-high heat. When the oil is shimmering, add the onion and a pinch of salt. Cook, stirring often, until the onion is soft and golden, about 7 minutes. Add the garlic, paprika, cumin, cinnamon, coriander and pepper flakes and stir for 30 seconds to let the spices bloom in the oil. Add the tomatoes, chickpeas, broth and pomegranate molasses and bring to a simmer. Turn off the heat and carefully spoon two-thirds of the tomato-chickpea mixture into a heatproof bowl.

Layer half the eggplant over the chickpea mixture in the pot and drizzle over 2 tablespoons (30 ml) of the remaining olive oil. Spread another third of the chickpeas over the eggplant. Layer on the rest of the eggplant, drizzle with the remaining oil and top with the last of the chickpea mixture. Cover and cook in the oven until the eggplant is very tender, about 1½ hours. Scatter the mint over the top and add a dollop of Greek yogurt to each serving, if desired. Serve hot over rice or couscous.

FOR THE POMEGRANATE MOLASSES (OPTIONAL)

4 cups (1 L) pomegranate juice

½ cup (100 g) sugar

2 tbsp (30 ml) lemon juice

FOR THE EGGPLANT

2 large or 3 medium eggplants (about 3 lbs [1.4 kg])

Kosher salt, as needed

6 tbsp (90 ml) extra-virgin olive oil, divided

1 large yellow onion, halved vertically and thinly sliced (just under 2 cups [320 g])

6 medium cloves garlic, minced

2 tsp (6 g) smoked paprika

2½ tsp (6 g) ground cumin

1½ tsp (4 g) ground cinnamon

½ tsp ground coriander

1 tsp crushed red pepper flakes

1 (28-oz [794-g]) can diced fire-roasted tomatoes

2 (16-oz [454-g]) cans chickpeas, drained and rinsed

1 cup (240 ml) vegetable broth, chicken stock or water

3 tbsp (45 ml) pomegranate molasses (or make your own: see directions)

½ cup (46 g) chopped fresh mint leaves

1 cup (240 ml) Greek yogurt (optional)

Rice or couscous, for serving

MISO-BRAISED CHARRED CABBAGE

Not enough encomiums are written in praise of the humble cabbage, and we think that's just wrong. This recipe proves that the braising technique doesn't only do wonders for cuts of meat, but also works its transformative magic on hardy greens. Braised cabbage becomes sweet and silky: the perfect foil for this garlicky, gingery braising sauce. Don't be afraid to let the cabbage get nice and dark, as that's where the best flavor lives.

¼ cup (70 g) white miso

½ cup (120 ml) sake or white wine

¼ cup (60 ml) mirin

3 large cloves garlic, minced or grated

1 tbsp (6 g) minced or grated fresh ginger

2 tsp (7 g) gochugaru or 1 tsp crushed red pepper flakes, plus extra for optional sprinkling

1 medium head of green or savoy cabbage (about 2 lbs [908 g])

3 tbsp (45 ml) neutral oil

Kosher salt, as needed

2 tsp (10 ml) toasted sesame oil

1 tbsp (9 g) white or black sesame seeds

¼ cup (25 g) chopped herbs (a combination of chives, cilantro, basil, shiso)

Preheat the oven to 350°F (180°C) and set a rack in the middle.

In a small bowl, mix together the miso, sake, mirin, garlic, ginger and gochugaru. Cut the cabbage in half through its core, then cut each half into four wedges, with the core holding each wedge intact. Heat the oil in a large Dutch oven set over medium-high heat. When the oil is shimmering, add the cabbage wedges to the pot, cut side down, and season them lightly with salt, working in batches as needed. Cook on one side until the cabbage is lightly charred, then flip and cook the other side, about 5 minutes per side. Add a little more oil if the pot looks dry. Transfer the cabbage to a plate.

Pour in the miso mixture and cook, stirring frequently, over medium heat for 2 minutes. Pour in 1½ cups (360 ml) of water and bring it to a simmer. Nestle the cabbage wedges back into the pot as best you can—a little overlap is fine. Transfer the pot to the oven and bake, uncovered, turning the wedges halfway through, until very tender, 30 to 40 minutes. If the liquid at the bottom of the pot has reduced and the pan starts getting dry before the cabbage is fully cooked, add a bit more water. To serve, drizzle the cabbage with sesame oil and sprinkle with sesame seeds and herbs (and gochugaru, if desired).

HONDASHI AND SAKE-BRAISED KABOCHA SQUASH

Kabocha squash, sometimes called Japanese pumpkin, is a delicious variety of winter squash, with sweet, nutty, deep-orange flesh and dark green edible skin. Our favorite way to prepare it is to braise it in a flavorful mix of hondashi (see Note below) and sake, seasoned with garlic and ginger. The liquid cooks down into a sweet-and-salty glaze that both infuses and coats the wedges of squash. If you can't find kabocha, the recipe works just as well with other winter squashes like delicata, butternut or acorn.

FOR THE HONDASHI

1 tsp hondashi granules (see Note)

1 cup (240 ml) hot water

½ cup (120 ml) sake or rice wine

¼ cup (60 ml) low-sodium soy sauce

¼ cup (60 ml) mirin

2 tbsp (28 g) brown sugar

1 tbsp (15 ml) rice vinegar

FOR THE SQUASH

½ large kabocha squash

2 tbsp (30 ml) vegetable oil

3 large cloves garlic, minced

1 tbsp (6 g) minced fresh ginger

4 scallions, whites cut into ½" (1.3-cm) pieces and greens thinly sliced, divided

1 tbsp (15 ml) toasted sesame oil

2 tsp (7 g) gochugaru or other chili flakes

1 tbsp (9 g) toasted sesame seeds

To make the hondashi, mix together the hondashi granules and hot water in a medium bowl. Stir in the sake, soy sauce, mirin, brown sugar and rice vinegar and set it aside.

To make the squash, microwave the whole kabocha on high power for 3 minutes to soften it enough to cut. Cut the kabocha in half through the stem, scrape out the seeds and cut one half into about eight wedges, each about 1½ inches (4 cm) thick. Save the other half of the squash for another recipe.

Heat the oil in a large Dutch oven over medium heat. When the oil is shimmering, add the squash wedges and cook, turning once, until they brown lightly on each side, 2 to 3 minutes per side. Work in batches as needed, then remove the squash slices to a plate and set them aside. Add the garlic, ginger and scallion whites to the pot and cook, stirring until the garlic turns fragrant, about 1 minute. Pour in the hondashi, add the squash back to the pot, nestling it in as best you can and bring the liquid to a simmer. Turn the heat to low, cover the pot and simmer for 10 minutes. Remove the lid, turn the wedges over and continue to cook, uncovered, until the squash is tender when pierced with a knife and the glaze has thickened, about 10 minutes. Remove the squash to a serving dish and pour over the remaining glaze, along with the sesame oil, gochugaru, sesame seeds and the reserved scallion greens.

NOTE: Hondashi is a type of Japanese bouillon, made from a smoked and dried fish called bonito. It adds a wonderful, smoky umami flavor, but you could substitute 1 cup (240 ml) of either chicken or vegetable stock. Look for it in the international aisle at your local grocery, at Asian markets or on the Internet.

SAUTÉS, BAKES AND STEAMS

Not all heroes wear capes, and not all Dutch oven dishes are slow-cooked. In fact, one of the quickest (and tastiest) recipes in this book is Brazilian-Style Collard Greens (*Couve à Mineira*) on page 54. Cut into the thinnest slivers, the greens are tossed in garlicky oil for mere minutes before they're ready for the table, and the Dutch oven's high sides make tossing a large mound of greens a breeze.

Speaking of breezes, let's pretend we're on a beach vacation. Have you ever steam-opened clams or mussels in your Dutch oven? The process for making Beer-Steamed Mussels with Chorizo and Fennel (page 53) is similar to that of a braise but takes almost no time at all. Mussels are tossed with browned sausage, sautéed vegetables and beer, and once the heavy lid goes on, the aromatic steam does all the work. All that's left to do is toast your bread for dunking.

Then there are the recipes that traditionally call for a full arsenal of pots and pans: often a skillet, a mixing bowl and a baking dish. As we were developing recipes for this book, it occurred to us that it was only habit that kept us working that way. The Dutch oven is ideal for all the steps in our Strata with Swiss Chard, Bacon and Leeks (page 58) and our Potato-Leek Gratin with Thyme (page 62), eliminating a mountain of washing up.

As you may have noticed, this chapter is all about variety: different techniques for dishes you can and should be making in your Dutch oven. If you haven't ventured past braising, now's your chance.

BEER-STEAMED MUSSELS
WITH CHORIZO AND FENNEL

There are very few foods that deliver as much bang for your buck as fresh-steamed mussels. They're cheap, sustainable and, when cooked properly, one of the most delicious proteins that can be plucked from the sea. In this dish, we combine the sweet, briny mussels with fresh fennel and spicy, smoky Spanish chorizo, which is a cured sausage that not only lends the broth great flavor, but also adds a gorgeous deep red color. If you're feeling adventurous, you could also make mussels' traditional accompaniment, Pommes Frites with Three Dipping Sauces (page 135).

In a large Dutch oven, heat the oil over medium heat until shimmering. Add the onion and fennel, season lightly with salt and pepper and cook, stirring frequently, until the vegetables are softened but not brown, 5 to 7 minutes. Add the chorizo and cook, stirring frequently, until it browns and releases some fat, about 5 minutes. Add the garlic and cook until it's fragrant, about 1 minute. Pour in the beer, increase the heat to high and bring it to a boil. Stir in the mussels, cover the pot and cook, shaking the pot occasionally until all the mussels are open, 2 to 4 minutes. Turn off the heat, add the reserved fennel fronds, parsley, lemon juice and zest and stir to combine. Taste the liquid, and adjust the seasoning with salt if needed. Discard any unopened mussels. Serve immediately with toasted bread, lemon wedges and a large bowl for the empty mussel shells.

2 tbsp (30 ml) extra-virgin olive oil

1 medium yellow onion, halved and thinly sliced pole to pole

1 medium fennel bulb, halved, cored and thinly sliced, fronds reserved

Kosher salt and freshly ground black pepper, as needed

6 oz (170 g) Spanish chorizo, chopped

4 medium cloves garlic, finely sliced

1 (12-oz [355-ml]) bottle blonde ale or wheat beer

2 lbs (908 g) mussels, scrubbed and debearded

¼ cup (15 g) chopped fresh parsley leaves

1 tbsp (15 ml) lemon juice

1 tsp finely grated lemon zest

1 baguette or ½ loaf rustic bread, thickly sliced, drizzled with olive oil and toasted

Lemon wedges, for serving

BRAZILIAN-STYLE COLLARD GREENS (COUVE À MINEIRA)

Unlike the long-simmered collard greens from the American South, the greens in this dish—from the Minas Gerais region of Brazil—are tenderized by being cut into very thin ribbons, then sautéed for just a few minutes with plenty of garlic and onion for flavor. It's the traditional accompaniment to feijoada (black bean stew), but it's a great side dish for just about everything. Use the high sides of your Dutch oven to really toss the greens around. We used to order this at our favorite Brazilian restaurant in Astoria while watching fútbol.

2 large bunches collard greens

3 tbsp (45 ml) extra-virgin olive oil or duck fat (see Crispy Braised Duck Legs with Lentils on page 23)

1 small yellow onion, finely diced

Pinch of kosher salt, plus more to taste

6 large cloves garlic, minced

1 lime, quartered for serving

Rinse the collard leaves and dry them well with paper towels. Trim the stems and cut out the large fibrous vein in the center of the collard leaf, cutting the leaf in half vertically. Stack a few leaves on top of one another and tightly roll them like a cigar. Slice them crosswise as thinly as possible. Repeat with the remaining leaves.

Heat the oil in a medium or large Dutch oven over medium heat. Add the onion and a good pinch of salt and sauté, stirring often, until soft and translucent, about 4 minutes. Add the garlic and cook for 1 minute. Turn the heat off and add the collard greens, folding and tossing them with tongs so the garlic gets mixed in with the greens. The residual heat should be enough to wilt the greens but not turn them mushy, 2 to 3 minutes. Transfer the collards to a serving bowl. Season with a squeeze of lime and more salt, to taste.

CRAB DIP-STUFFED ARTICHOKES

Thistles aren't just beautiful, they're also edible—in the form of artichokes. Sure, you can dip the leaves in butter or flavored mayonnaise and it'll be tasty, but for a real indulgence, we hollow out the centers and fill them with a decadent crab dip. A Dutch oven serves as the perfect vessel both for steaming the artichokes and for baking them once they're stuffed with dip. The combination of sweet artichoke and spicy, creamy crab dip? Chef's kiss.

To prep the artichokes, pull off any tough or marred outer leaves. Using a sharp, serrated knife, cut off the top third of each artichoke. Trim any remaining sharp or spiky tips with kitchen scissors. Trim the stems enough so the artichokes will sit flat when they're baked. As you work, rub any cut surfaces with lemon to keep them from browning.

Set a steamer basket in a large Dutch oven and add enough water so it reaches just below the basket. (If you don't have a steamer basket, a few crumpled up balls of aluminum foil work just as well.) Squeeze in the juice from 1 lemon and add the salt. Bring the water to a boil and arrange the artichokes in the steamer stem side up. Cover the pot and steam until the hearts are tender when pierced with a tip of a paring knife and the inner leaves pull out easily, 25 to 35 minutes. Remove the artichokes and set them aside until they are cool enough to handle. Pour the water out of the Dutch oven.

Preheat the oven to 375°F (190°C) and set a rack in the middle.

To make the dip, stir together the cream cheese, sour cream and mayonnaise in a medium bowl until completely combined. Stir in the cheddar cheese, garlic, Worcestershire, lemon juice, hot sauce and mustard powder. Season with salt and pepper, to taste, and gently fold in the crabmeat, being careful not to break it up too much.

Pull out the soft center leaves of each artichoke to reveal the fuzzy choke. Use a spoon to scrape away and remove the choke, leaving a hole in the center of each artichoke. Nestle the artichokes back into the Dutch oven, hole side up, making sure they stand upright. Evenly divide the crab dip between the artichokes, spooning it into the centers. Sprinkle the tops with the breadcrumbs, season them with a little salt and pepper and drizzle a little olive oil to moisten the crumbs. Place the pot in the oven, uncovered, and bake until the dip is hot and bubbly and the crumb topping is golden brown, 10 to 15 minutes. Remove from the oven, sprinkle them with the chives and serve hot.

FOR THE ARTICHOKES

4–6 large globe artichokes

2 lemons, 1 halved to rub on the artichokes and 1 for juice

1 tbsp (8 g) kosher salt

FOR THE CRAB DIP

8 oz (227 g) cream cheese, room temperature

¼ cup (60 ml) sour cream

¼ cup (60 ml) mayonnaise

1 cup (113 g) grated sharp cheddar cheese

2 large cloves garlic, grated or minced

1 tbsp (15 ml) Worcestershire sauce

1 tbsp (15 ml) lemon juice

2 tsp (10 ml) hot sauce, plus more to taste

½ tsp dry mustard powder

Kosher salt and freshly ground black pepper, to taste

1 lb (454 g) lump crabmeat, picked over for shells

½ cup (28 g) fresh breadcrumbs or panko

Extra-virgin olive oil, for drizzling

2 tbsp (6 g) minced chives or 2 chopped scallions

STRATA WITH SWISS CHARD, BACON AND LEEKS

A strata is essentially a savory bread pudding, and it's perfect for breakfast, lunch or dinner. You can flavor it a million different ways, but we usually stick to a simple flavor trifecta. There's always some kind of allium, in this case leeks, sautéed until they turn tender and sweet. We add greens: often our favorite, Swiss chard, though spinach and kale are also great. And bacon . . . because bacon! Oh, and cheese. Okay, so less a trifecta than a mélange. It's a great way to use up bits of vegetables that you might have left over from other recipes, and it also happens to be the tastiest make-ahead breakfast we know.

1 (1-lb [454-g]) rustic country loaf, cut into 2" (5-cm) cubes (or use Basic Dutch Oven No-Knead Bread on page 125)

10 large eggs

2 cups (480 ml) whole milk or half-and-half

½ cup (120 ml) crème fraîche or sour cream

¼ tsp freshly grated nutmeg

Kosher salt and freshly ground black pepper, as needed

10 oz (283 g) thick-cut bacon (about 8 rashers), cut into 1" (2.5-cm) pieces

2 tbsp (28 g) unsalted butter

3 large leeks, white and pale-green parts only, rinsed and thinly sliced

1 large bunch (about ½ lb [227 g]) Swiss chard, tender stems finely sliced and leaves roughly chopped

½ cup (120 ml) dry white wine

2 oz (57 g) Gruyère or sharp cheddar cheese, grated and divided

Preheat the oven to 250°F (120°C) and set a rack in the middle.

Arrange the bread cubes in a single layer on a rimmed baking sheet and bake until the bread turns dry and crisp, about 30 minutes, tossing the cubes halfway through baking. Remove them from the oven and set them aside. In a large bowl, whisk together the eggs, milk, crème fraîche and the nutmeg. Season with a good pinch of salt and pepper, then add the bread cubes and toss until the bread is coated. Cover the bowl with plastic wrap and refrigerate it for at least 30 minutes, tossing the cubes occasionally to make sure they evenly absorb the custard.

Raise the oven temperature to 325°F (165°C).

Add the bacon to a large Dutch oven and turn the heat on medium. Cook, tossing occasionally, until the bacon turns crisp and golden brown, 5 to 7 minutes. Remove the bacon with a slotted spoon to a paper towel–lined plate and set it aside. Remove all but 1 tablespoon (15 ml) of the bacon fat and add the butter. When the butter has melted, add the leeks and the chard stems, season with salt and pepper and cook until they soften, about 7 minutes. Add the wine and simmer until it has reduced by half, about 3 minutes. Add the chard leaves and stir until wilted, 2 minutes. Remove the pot from the heat, pour in the bread-custard mix, the bacon and half the cheese and toss until everything is combined. Sprinkle the top with the remaining cheese. Bake until the center is puffed, the top is golden and the edges have pulled slightly away from the sides of the pot, 50 to 60 minutes. Let it cool for 5 minutes before serving.

NOTE: The strata can be made up to 2 days ahead. Cover the assembled but un-baked strata with plastic wrap (or the Dutch oven lid) and refrigerate until you're ready to bake.

THAI-STYLE TURKEY MEATBALLS
IN COCONUT RED CURRY

This Thai-influenced dish delivers big flavor for very little work. We mix ground turkey (or chicken, if you like, but please use dark meat) with lots of ginger, garlic, cilantro and scallions. Once the meatballs have been baked golden brown, off they go into the pot filled with a delicious coconut milk–based red curry sauce. The flavor is so vibrant, the meatballs need only a quick toss in the sauce and they're ready. Just before serving, we wilt in some baby spinach and give the whole dish a shower of bright herbs straight from the garden (or grocery store).

Preheat the oven to 400°F (200°C) and place a rack in the middle. Line a rimmed baking sheet with foil or parchment.

To make the meatballs, add the turkey, breadcrumbs, scallions, cilantro, ginger, garlic, eggs, fish sauce and salt to a large bowl and, using your fingers or a fork, gently mix everything together until fully combined. Don't squeeze the meat, or the meatballs will be dense. Use about 2 tablespoons (30 g) of the mixture to form each ball, and arrange them on the baking sheet with a little space between each. Bake the meatballs until golden brown and just cooked through, 12 to 14 minutes. Remove the sheet from the oven and set aside.

While the meatballs are cooking, make the curry sauce. Heat the oil over medium-high heat in a medium or large Dutch oven. Add the onion and cook, stirring often, until it turns soft and translucent, 5 to 7 minutes. Stir in the garlic and ginger and cook until fragrant, about 1 minute. Add the red curry paste and cook, stirring everything around, until the paste sizzles and turns a darker red, about 3 minutes. Stir in the coconut milk, chicken stock, fish sauce, brown sugar and peanut butter and bring to a boil, then lower the heat and gently simmer until the sauce thickens slightly, about 5 minutes. Add the spinach and lime juice and stir until the leaves are wilted, 1 minute. Transfer the meatballs to the pot and gently toss until they're coated in the sauce. Serve on top of rice or rice noodles with lots of fresh herbs and lime wedges for squeezing.

FOR THE MEATBALLS

2 lbs (908 g) ground turkey or chicken, dark meat recommended

½ cup (28 g) panko breadcrumbs

3 medium scallions, minced (about ¼ cup [12 g])

3 tbsp (3 g) finely chopped cilantro, plus more for garnish

1 tbsp (6 g) fresh minced or grated ginger

3 large cloves garlic, minced or grated

2 large eggs

1 tbsp (15 ml) fish sauce

1 tsp kosher salt, as needed

FOR THE CURRY

1 tbsp (15 ml) coconut or neutral oil

1 large yellow onion, finely chopped (about 1½ cups [240 g])

3 large cloves garlic, minced or grated

2 tbsp (12 g) minced or grated fresh ginger

3 tbsp (48 g) red curry paste, or more if you like spicy

1 (13.5-oz [400-ml]) can coconut milk

½ cup (120 ml) Golden Chicken Stock (page 84) or store-bought stock

1 tbsp (15 ml) fish sauce

1 tbsp (14 g) brown sugar

2 tbsp (32 g) smooth peanut butter

3 cups (90 g) baby spinach

1 tbsp (15 ml) lime juice

Steamed rice or rice noodles, for serving

Roughly chopped fresh mint, basil and/or cilantro leaves, for garnish

Lime wedges, for serving

POTATO-LEEK GRATIN
WITH THYME

American fans of good ole cheesy scalloped potatoes might be surprised to know that this dish was born of the French technique known as gratiné: the forming of a crust. Many such recipes call for cooking the potatoes and sauce in separate pans, then combining them in a gratin dish before baking in the oven. We streamline the process by cooking everything that can then be presented to the table—leeks, bechamel sauce and potatoes—in the Dutch oven. It makes a spectacular Thanksgiving side dish, though the other 364 days might get jealous if you only make it once a year.

6 tbsp (84 g) unsalted butter

5 large leeks, white and pale-green parts, rinsed and thinly sliced

Kosher salt and freshly ground black pepper, as needed

4 large cloves garlic, minced or grated

¾ cup (180 ml) dry white wine

6 tbsp (48 g) all-purpose flour

3½ cups (840 ml) whole milk

1 cup (240 ml) crème fraîche

1 tbsp (2 g) fresh thyme leaves, from about 10 sprigs

¼ tsp freshly grated nutmeg

4 lbs (1.8 kg) Yukon Gold or russet potatoes, peeled and very thinly sliced (see Note)

4 oz (113 g) Gruyère or sharp cheddar cheese, grated

Preheat the oven to 375°F (190°C) and set a rack in the middle. Line a rimmed baking sheet with foil.

Melt the butter in a medium or large Dutch oven set over medium heat. Add the leeks and a good pinch of salt and pepper. Cook, stirring often, until the leeks soften, 5 to 7 minutes. Add the garlic and cook until fragrant, 1 minute. Add the wine and cook, stirring occasionally, until the wine has mostly evaporated, about 3 minutes. Whisk in the flour and cook, whisking constantly, until the leeks are coated, about 2 minutes. Slowly whisk in the milk 1 cup (240 ml) at a time, making sure there are no lumps of flour before adding more. Turn off the heat and stir in the crème fraîche, thyme leaves and nutmeg. Season the sauce to taste with salt and pepper. You should have about 5 cups (1.2 L) of sauce in total.

Using a ladle, remove all but 1 cup (240 ml) of the sauce to a bowl and set it aside. In the pot, on top of the sauce in the Dutch oven, arrange about one-quarter of the potato slices (about 1 pound [454 g]) in roughly a single layer, though some overlapping and doubling up is fine. Season the potatoes lightly with salt and pepper, then spread another 1 cup (240 ml) of the sauce on top. Repeat three times for a total of four layers of potatoes, and end with a final layer of sauce, seasoning each layer of potatoes with salt and pepper. Place the pot on the foil-lined baking sheet, cover it with the lid and bake for 1 hour. Remove the lid, sprinkle the top evenly with the cheese and bake, uncovered, until the potatoes are fully tender and the top is golden brown and bubbling, about 30 minutes. Remove the pot from the oven, and let it rest for at least 10 minutes before serving.

NOTE: A mandoline set at ⅛" (3-mm) thickness is the best way to slice the potatoes quickly and evenly. If you don't have one, a sharp knife will work fine, it will just take a little longer. To prevent the sliced potatoes from turning brown, keep them in a bowl of cold water. When you're ready to use them, drain them and pat them dry.

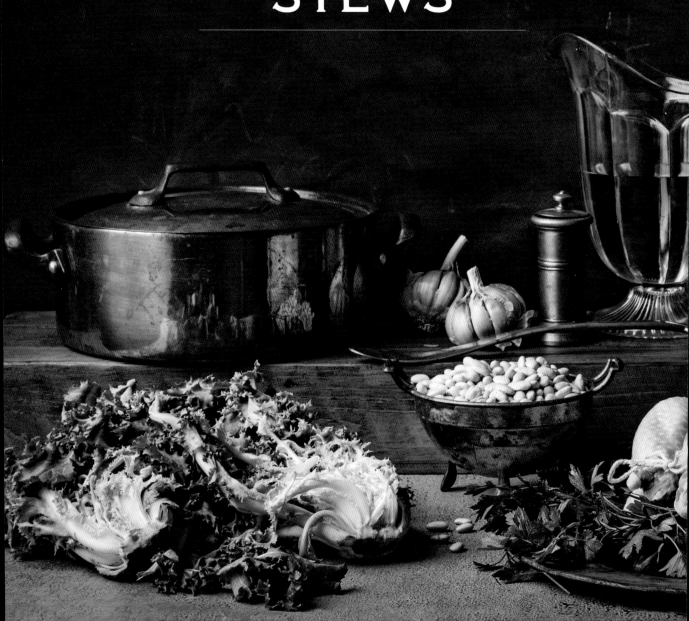

SOUPS AND STEWS

The Dutch oven excels at making soups and stews for many of the same reasons it's your best friend for braising: the heavy bottom is a great base to sauté or sear the component ingredients, and the oven's multi-quart volume and high sides give you a sturdy stockpot that'll hold whatever you put in it.

Here, you'll find a wide range of soups and stews that demonstrate the versatility of the Dutch oven as a cooking pot. The best soups start with a flavorful stock, and we give you recipes for Golden Chicken Stock (page 84) as well as our Rich Vegetable Broth (page 87), which create the basis for many of the recipes elsewhere in the book. If you've ever wondered why certain dishes at restaurants taste better than home-cooked versions, the reason is probably the stock.

Tortellini en Brodo with Spinach (page 67) takes this stock, and with minimal additions, delivers a quick, simple soup to rival any restaurant consommé.

Building a flavor base can involve sautéing vegetables, such as the mirepoix of onions, carrots, celery and garlic that we use in Baked Ribollita (page 75); toasting spices, as in Green Chicken Chili (page 80); or roasting meat, as in Jamaican-Style Oxtail and Butter Bean Stew (page 79). This deepens and combines the component elements in a way that is simply impossible if ingredients are simply chopped and thrown into hot water.

What exactly the difference is between a soup and a stew is mostly defined by the amount of liquid the recipes contain, with stews having less liquid by volume than soup. Stews also tend to call for larger cuts of meat and vegetables, with liquid that gets cooked down and thickened. (There is a lot of crossover between a soup, a stew or, for that matter, a braise. As long as you enjoy it, you shouldn't worry too much about the terminology!)

There's no good reason to crowd your stovetop with both a sauté pan and a separate stockpot. And because the iron walls of a Dutch oven spread heat out efficiently, it becomes much easier to control the soup's simmer once you bring it to temperature. (As our grandmothers always told us, a soup boiled is a soup spoiled.)

TORTELLINI EN BRODO
WITH SPINACH

Tortellini en Brodo is classically a first course but can be made into a meal with not a lot of trouble. Source a good frozen tortellini, unless you want to make your own, but you'll definitely want to use one of the homemade stocks at the end of this chapter — Golden Chicken Stock (page 84) or Rich Vegetable Broth (page 87). Note that cooking the pasta separately keeps the broth from becoming cloudy.

Bring the water to a boil in a medium saucepan. Add the salt and cook the tortellini according to the package directions. Drain through a colander, and then rinse with water and set aside.

While the pasta is cooking, heat the oil in a 3-quart (3-L) or larger Dutch oven set over medium heat. When the oil is shimmering, add the leeks and cook, stirring often, until they turn soft and translucent but not brown, 5 to 7 minutes. Add the stock and the Parmigiano-Reggiano rind, if using, and bring to a bare simmer, turning the heat lower as needed. Add the beans and simmer for about 5 minutes, and then add the cooked tortellini and continue to simmer until the tortellini are hot, about 2 minutes. Add the spinach, and stir until it wilts, 1 minute. Taste and adjust the seasoning as needed. Remove the rind, divide among soup bowls and grate a little Parmigiano-Reggiano over each.

4 qt (4 L) water

2 tbsp (16 g) kosher salt, plus more to taste

1 (9-oz [255-g]) package frozen cheese or meat tortellini

1 tbsp (15 ml) extra-virgin olive oil

2 small leeks, white and pale-green parts only, rinsed, halved lengthwise and thinly sliced

6 cups (1.4 L) Golden Chicken Stock (page 84), Rich Vegetable Broth (page 87) or other good-quality stock

1 small piece Parmigiano-Reggiano rind (optional)

1 (15-oz [425-g]) can cannellini beans, drained and rinsed

6 cups (180 g) baby spinach

Parmigiano-Reggiano, for serving

WONTON SOUP
WITH HOMEMADE DUMPLINGS AND BOK CHOY

Feel a little sniffle coming on? Get some wonton soup in you. Long day at work? Soup will help. Somehow that magical combination of hot, gingery chicken broth and silky-yet-hearty dumplings makes everything feel just a little bit better. Yes, folding the dumplings by hand is a little time consuming, but it's also very easy and the results are absolutely worth it.

To make the broth, add the chicken stock, pancetta, if using, ginger, kombu, wine, soy sauce, garlic and scallions to a large Dutch oven. Bring it to a boil, then turn the heat down to low and gently simmer for at least 30 minutes.

While the broth is simmering, make the wontons. Finely chop the shrimp (or pulse them in a food processor) and add them to a medium bowl. Add the pork, ginger, garlic, sugar, soy sauce, Shaoxing wine, sesame oil, scallions, cornstarch and salt. Gently mix with your fingers, chopsticks or a spoon until thoroughly combined.

Set a small bowl of water next to a clean cutting board. Place 1 wonton wrapper in the center of the board, keeping the rest covered with a slightly damp cloth or paper towel. Place about 1½ teaspoons (7 g) of the filling in the center of the wrapper. Using your fingertip, moisten the wrapper with water all around the edge. Fold two opposite corners up to make a triangle, and press the edges together to form a tight seal. Pull the two opposite corners of the triangle towards each other to form a crescent shape, using a little more water to seal the edges. Transfer each completed wonton to a rimmed baking tray, and cover them with a very lightly moistened kitchen towel to keep them from drying out as you work.

Once the wontons are assembled, remove and discard all the solids (except the pancetta, if using) from the broth, using tongs or a spoon. Bring the broth back to a simmer. Add the wontons and the bok choy, and cook until the wontons are cooked through, about 4 minutes. Stir in the sliced scallions, taste the broth and season with salt as desired. Optionally, drizzle in a little chili oil or chili-garlic paste, to taste.

NOTE: Both the broth and the wontons can be made ahead and frozen. To freeze the wontons, place them on a parchment-lined sheet tray, cover them loosely with plastic wrap and place the tray in the freezer until they are completely frozen, about 1 hour. Transfer them to a freezer bag. They can be cooked directly from frozen. Just add 1 to 2 minutes to the cooking time.

FOR THE BROTH

2 qt (2 L) Golden Chicken Stock (page 84) or store-bought stock

4 oz (113 g) pancetta, cut into thin 1" (2.5-cm)-long strips (optional)

1 (4" [10-cm]) knob fresh ginger, cut into 3 or 4 long slices

1 (4" [10-cm]) piece of kombu (optional)

2 tbsp (30 ml) Shaoxing wine or dry sherry

1 tbsp (15 ml) light soy sauce

3 medium cloves garlic, peeled and smashed

4 scallions, root end trimmed, cut in half

Kosher salt, to taste

FOR THE WONTONS

½ lb (227 g) medium shrimp, peeled and deveined

½ lb (227 g) ground pork

1 tbsp (6 g) grated fresh ginger

1 large clove garlic, grated

1 tsp sugar

1 tbsp (15 ml) light soy sauce

2 tbsp (30 ml) Shaoxing wine or dry sherry

1 tbsp (15 ml) sesame oil

4 scallions or 1 small bunch Chinese chives, very finely minced

1 tsp cornstarch

1 tsp kosher salt

24 to 30 fresh wonton wrappers

FOR SERVING

8 small baby bok choy, cut in half vertically

2 scallions, finely sliced

Chili oil or chili-garlic paste (optional)

TADKA DAL

Dal—a thick, spiced dish made from pulses—is an essential part of Indian cuisine and one of Matt's favorite curried recipes. You can use a wide range of dried peas or beans, such as mung beans or chickpeas, but we like split red lentils, which can be easily found in American groceries. There are layers of seasoning in this dish: The dal itself is spiced with garlic and ginger and is further enhanced by the tadka—a mix of golden fried onions and quick-cooked whole spices that get added in just before serving.

To make the dal, soak the lentils for 30 minutes, then rinse and drain them. In a large Dutch oven over medium heat, melt the ghee. Add the onions and salt and cook, stirring frequently, until the onions are soft and just starting to turn a little brown, 10 to 15 minutes. Don't rush this step! Add the garlic and ginger and cook until aromatic, 1 to 2 minutes. Add the lentils and turmeric and stir to combine, then add the water. Bring to a boil, then turn the heat down to a simmer and cook, covered, for 30 minutes, stirring occasionally.

When the lentils are almost fully tender, prepare the tadka. In a small sauté pan set over medium heat, melt the ghee and add the sliced onion, cooking for 5 to 10 minutes, stirring occasionally. Add the garlic, mustard seed, coriander seed, curry powder and whole red chilis. Toast the spices for 1 to 2 minutes. Spoon a little of the hot lentil mix into the tadka, stir to combine, then return the combination back to the lentil pot and stir it in. Serve with warm buttered naan bread and cilantro.

FOR THE DAL

5 cups (960 g) washed split red lentils

2 tbsp (28 g) ghee or clarified butter

2 medium onions, finely chopped

2 tsp (6 g) kosher salt, divided

4 cloves garlic, finely chopped

1 (2" [5-cm]) piece fresh ginger, grated

1 tsp ground turmeric

7 cups (1.7 L) water

FOR THE TADKA

3 tbsp (42 g) ghee or clarified butter

1 medium onion, sliced pole-to-pole

1 clove garlic, sliced

1 tbsp (6 g) mustard seed

1 tbsp (6 g) coriander seed

1 tbsp (6 g) curry powder

3 dried red chile peppers, left whole but seeds removed

FOR SERVING

Naan bread

Fresh cilantro

SMOKY AND CREAMY CORN CHOWDER
WITH SHRIMP

Making corn chowder is our favorite way to ease into early autumn, when there's still farm-fresh corn at the market but the colder evenings have us craving something cozy for supper. This chowder combines sweet corn and smoky bacon in a creamy broth, dotted with lightly poached shrimp, silky potatoes and sliced jalapeños to soothe the end-of-summer blues.

In a medium bowl, toss the shrimp with the salt and baking soda. Cover with plastic wrap and refrigerate for at least 15 minutes and up to 1 hour.

Stand a corn cob on its wider end in a large bowl. Using a sharp knife, slice the kernels from the cob. Repeat with the other cobs and set the bowl aside. In a small bowl, run the back of the knife firmly against the cobs to scrape any pulp and milk into the bowl; you should end up with about 1 cup (240 ml) of pulp.

Add the bacon to a large Dutch oven and set it over medium-high heat. Cook until the bacon turns crisp and golden brown, 5 to 7 minutes. Use a slotted spoon to remove the bacon to a paper towel–lined plate and set it aside. Reduce the heat to medium-low, add the leeks and cook, stirring often, until softened, about 5 minutes. Add the garlic and jalapeño and sauté until fragrant, about 1 minute. Add the sherry and cook until it evaporates, about 2 minutes. Stir in the flour and cook, stirring constantly, for 2 minutes. While whisking constantly, gradually add the stock and milk and bring to a boil. Add the potatoes, bay leaf, thyme, corn pulp and cream cheese. Bring to a boil. Reduce the heat to medium-low and simmer until the potatoes are almost fork tender, 8 to 10 minutes. Add the corn kernels, return to a simmer and cook for 5 minutes. Add the shrimp and simmer until they are opaque and just cooked through, 3 to 5 minutes. Discard the bay leaf. Season with salt and pepper to taste. Ladle into serving bowls, and sprinkle each bowl with some scallions, bacon and a couple of jalapeño slices.

1 lb (454 g) medium shrimp, peeled and deveined

1 tsp kosher salt, plus more to taste

¼ tsp baking soda

6 ears corn (about 4½ cups [693 g] of kernels), husks and silks removed

5 slices (about 7 oz [198 g]) thick-cut smoked bacon, chopped into 1" (2.5-cm) pieces

2 large leeks, white and pale-green parts only, cleaned and chopped

4 medium cloves garlic, minced

1 jalapeño, ribs and seeds removed, finely chopped, plus a few thin slices for garnish

¼ cup (60 ml) dry sherry or white wine

3 tbsp (24 g) all-purpose flour

3 cups (720 ml) Golden Chicken Stock (page 84) or store-bought stock

2½ cups (600 ml) whole milk or half-and-half

¾ lb (340 g) red potatoes, scrubbed and cut into 1" (2.5-cm) cubes (about 2 cups [300 g])

1 bay leaf

1 tsp minced fresh thyme leaves or ¼ tsp dried

3 oz (85 g) cream cheese, room temperature

Freshly ground black pepper, to taste

2 scallions, finely sliced, for garnish

BAKED RIBOLLITA

The term ribollita refers more to a technique than it does a specific recipe. It's the act of preparing a soup or stew in advance and reheating it a second time or even several times. It has become a symbol of Tuscan cuisine, and all the ingredients are prized in the area: Tuscan kale (called black cabbage in Italy), cannellini beans, fresh herbs and good bread. Like many great recipes, ribollita is founded on the tradition of, "non buttar via niente," which means, "don't throw away anything!" What you toss in the pot is up to you, but the finishing touches of good crusty bread and lots of high-quality olive oil are essential.

Preheat the oven to 450°F (230°C), and place a rack in the middle.

Heat the oil in a large Dutch oven set over medium heat. When the oil is shimmering, add the onion, carrots, celery, salt and pepper. Cook, stirring occasionally, until the vegetables are softened but not browned, 8 to 10 minutes. Add the garlic and tomato paste and cook, stirring frequently, until the garlic is fragrant, about 2 minutes. Add the crushed tomatoes along with any juices, and use a wooden spoon to scrape any browned bits off the bottom of the pot. Add the stock, rosemary and thyme. If you're using it, add the rind to the pot. Add the beans and red pepper flakes. Bring the liquid to a boil, lower it to a simmer and let it cook, stirring occasionally, for 15 minutes. Remove the rind, and begin adding the kale, a handful at a time, stirring it in until it wilts before adding more until it's all in the pot. Repeat the process with the chard.

Add about one-third of the bread and stir it in until it's submerged and soaked in broth. Taste the broth and adjust the seasoning with salt and pepper. Place the remaining bread chunks on top of the stew, drizzle them generously with olive oil and add half the Parmigiano-Reggiano on top. Transfer the pot to the oven, and bake, uncovered, until the bread is golden brown on top and the stew is bubbling gloriously, 10 to 15 minutes. Ladle the stew into serving bowls, drizzle each with more olive oil and add the remaining Parmigiano-Reggiano over the top.

⅓ cup (80 ml) extra-virgin olive oil, plus more for drizzling

1 large Spanish onion, diced

3 medium carrots, peeled and diced

2 celery ribs, diced

2 tsp (6 g) kosher salt, plus more to taste

½ tsp freshly ground black pepper, plus more to taste

8 large cloves garlic, minced

2 tbsp (32 g) tomato paste

1 (28-oz [794-g]) can whole peeled tomatoes, crushed by hand into small pieces

5 cups (1.2 L) Rich Vegetable Broth (page 87), Golden Chicken Stock (page 84) or water

1 tsp minced fresh rosemary

2 tsp (1 g) minced fresh thyme

1 small piece Parmigiano-Reggiano rind (optional)

2 (15-oz [425-g]) cans cannellini beans, drained and rinsed

½ tsp crushed red pepper flakes

1 bunch Tuscan kale, tough stems discarded and leaves torn into 2" (5-cm) pieces

1 bunch Swiss chard, tough stems discarded and leaves torn into 2" (5-cm) pieces

½ loaf crusty country bread (about 10 oz [283 g]), torn into ragged 2" (5-cm) pieces, for serving

1 cup (100 g) freshly grated Parmigiano-Reggiano, divided

CREAMY CHICKEN STEW AND CHIVE DUMPLINGS

Our version of this classic recipe results in tender chicken; a rich and creamy broth; and chive-flecked, light-as-air dumplings. While not traditional, popping the pot under the broiler for a few minutes gives the dumplings a beautiful golden brown crust, a great contrast to their pillowy center. This is Southern fine dining.

To make the stew, melt the butter in a large Dutch oven set over medium heat. Add the onion, celery and carrots, season with salt and pepper and cook, stirring often, until the vegetables are softened but not browned, 8 minutes. Add the garlic and cook until fragrant, 1 minute. Add the stock, thyme, bay leaf and chicken, making sure all the chicken pieces are submerged. Bring the liquid to a full boil, cover the pot, turn the heat down to low and simmer for 10 minutes. Turn off the heat and let the chicken continue to poach in the hot broth for 10 minutes. Transfer the chicken to a plate and let it sit until cool enough to handle. Shred the meat and cover with foil to keep it warm. Set it aside.

Add the flour to a small bowl and whisk in the evaporated milk until the mixture is completely smooth. Turn the heat under the Dutch oven back to low and slowly pour the milk-flour mixture into the chicken stock, whisking constantly. Add the cream cheese, stirring until it melts. Add the shredded chicken back to the pot and let it simmer, stirring occasionally, while you make the dumpling dough.

To make the dumplings, in a medium bowl, whisk together the flour, baking powder, baking soda, salt and pepper. In a small bowl, stir together the buttermilk, butter and chives. Slowly pour the buttermilk mixture into the dry ingredients, stirring just until the dough comes together. Be careful not to overmix it, or the dumplings will be tough.

Drop tablespoon-sized (15-g) dollops of dumpling dough on top of the stew, leaving a little room between each one. Cover and simmer for 10 to 12 minutes. The dumplings should have grown in size by roughly fivefold, and the interior should look like a soft dinner roll. If they're not fully cooked, cover and cook for 2 minutes more. If you like browned dumplings like we do, preheat your broiler while the dumplings are poaching. Once the dumplings are puffed, place the pot in the oven, uncovered, and broil until their tops are golden brown, 2 to 5 minutes, depending on your broiler. Divide the chicken stew and dumplings among bowls, and top with more chives, if desired.

FOR THE STEW

4 tbsp (56 g) unsalted butter

1 large yellow or Spanish onion, diced

2 celery ribs, diced

3 medium carrots, diced

Kosher salt and freshly ground black pepper, as needed

4 cloves garlic, minced

6 cups (1.4 L) Golden Chicken Stock (page 84) or store-bought stock

1 tsp minced fresh thyme leaves

1 bay leaf

3 lbs (1.4 kg) boneless, skinless chicken thighs or breasts

6 tbsp (48 g) all-purpose flour

1 (12-oz [355-ml]) can evaporated milk

4 oz (113 g) cream cheese, room temperature, cut into cubes

FOR THE DUMPLINGS

1 cup (125 g) all-purpose flour

2 tsp (6 g) baking powder

¼ tsp baking soda

1 tsp kosher salt

¼ tsp freshly ground black pepper

½ cup plus 2 tbsp (150 g) buttermilk

3 tbsp (45 ml) melted unsalted butter, cooled

¼ cup (12 g) finely minced fresh chives, plus more for garnish

JAMAICAN-STYLE OXTAIL AND BUTTER BEAN STEW

Oxtails are cooked around the world and are a particular staple in Caribbean cuisine. The origins of this dish date from the one-pot cooking traditions used by enslaved Africans as early as the mid-1500s. Jamaica's unique culinary heritage developed from the variety of cultures that inhabited the island over the years, resulting in dishes like this stew, packed with distinctive flavor from allspice and fiery Scotch bonnet chiles. Once considered a throwaway cut of beef, oxtails are extremely high in gelatin, so a low-and-slow braise turns the meat particularly luscious.

At least 1 hour before you plan to serve them, dry the oxtails with paper towels and sprinkle them generously with salt on all sides. Leave to season at room temperature for the hour, or place them in a bowl covered with plastic wrap and store them in the refrigerator for up to 2 days.

When ready to cook, preheat the oven to 425°F (220°C) and place a rack on the lower middle shelf.

Add the oxtails in a single layer to a roasting pan or rimmed baking sheet, season generously with pepper and roast, turning halfway through, until the pieces are brown and crusty, 30 to 40 minutes. Once the oxtails are roasted, set them aside and lower the oven temperature to 275°F (135°C).

While the beef is roasting, prepare the braising liquid. Heat a large Dutch oven over medium heat and add the olive oil. When the oil is shimmering, add the onion, carrots, celery and red bell pepper, season with salt and pepper and cook, stirring often, until the vegetables become tender, 7 to 10 minutes. Add the garlic and cook until fragrant, about 1 minute. Sprinkle over the flour and stir until it fully coats the vegetables. Stir in the wine, stock and vinegar and use a wooden spoon to scrape up any brown bits. Add the ketchup, tomato paste, brown sugar, Worcestershire sauce, soy sauce, allspice, bay leaves and thyme. Take the Scotch bonnet or habanero and, using a sharp paring knife, cut thin slits along each side of the chile. Add it to the pot.

Transfer the roasted oxtails to the pot, nestling them so they are mostly submerged in liquid. Turn the heat up to medium-high, bring the liquid up to a boil and then cover the pot and place it in the oven. Cook until the meat is falling-off-the-bone tender, 3 to 3½ hours. Check every hour to make sure the beef remains mostly submerged in liquid, adding stock or water if needed. Add the butter beans 30 minutes from the end of cooking time. Remove the pot from the oven and let it sit for at least 15 minutes. Spoon off as much fat as you can from the top and remove the bay leaves and thyme sprigs. Taste the sauce and season with salt and pepper as needed. Serve the oxtails hot, over rice or mashed potatoes.

3–4 lbs (1.4–1.8 kg) oxtails, trimmed of excess fat if necessary

Kosher salt and freshly ground black pepper, as needed

2 tbsp (30 ml) extra-virgin olive oil

1 large Spanish onion, diced

2 large carrots, peeled and diced

2 celery ribs, diced

1 red bell pepper, seeded and diced

5 large cloves garlic, minced

2 tbsp (16 g) all-purpose flour

2 cups (480 ml) dry red wine

1 cup (240 ml) Golden Chicken Stock (page 84) or beef stock, plus more as needed

¼ cup (60 ml) apple cider vinegar

1 cup (240 ml) ketchup

2 tbsp (32 g) tomato paste

¼ cup (56 g) light brown sugar

2 tbsp (30 ml) Worcestershire sauce

1 tbsp (15 ml) soy sauce

1 tbsp (6 g) ground allspice

3 bay leaves

4 sprigs fresh thyme

1 Scotch bonnet or habanero pepper

1 (15-oz [425-g]) can butter beans, drained and rinsed

Rice or mashed potatoes, for serving

GREEN CHICKEN CHILI

While beef chilis employ a base of chili powder and tomato (which creates its classic brown color), the chicken version uses creamy cannellini beans and is usually known as white chili. We're calling our version green chili since we gleefully toss in handfuls of chopped cilantro. The fresh chile peppers we add are mostly on the mild side, but they do supply a lot of flavor, especially once they're roasted. If you like to live life on the spicy side, add an extra jalapeño or two and leave the seeds in.

Preheat the broiler to high and place an oven rack about 8 inches (20 cm) below the broiler element.

Place the Anaheims, poblanos, jalapeños, onion and garlic on a sheet tray and drizzle them with 1 tablespoon (15 ml) of the oil. Use your hands to make sure everything is coated, then season with salt. Place the tray under the broiler and cook, turning the peppers occasionally, until they are charred on all sides and the skins are blistered, 15 to 20 minutes. Transfer everything to a heatproof bowl and cover tightly with plastic wrap. Let everything rest for 10 minutes. Once cool, move the peppers to a cutting board and, using your hands, rub off the skins and scrape away as many seeds as possible. Roughly chop the peppers and add them to the bowl of a food processor or blender, along with the broiled onion and garlic. Add 1 cup (262 g) of the beans. Blend until a smooth puree is formed. Set aside.

Heat the remaining oil in a large Dutch oven set over medium heat and add the cumin and coriander. Cook, stirring, until fragrant, about 30 seconds. Add the chili-bean mixture and cook, stirring, for 2 minutes. Stir in the chicken stock and the remaining beans. Bring the liquid to a boil and then lower the temperature to a simmer. Stir in half of the pepper Jack until it has melted, about 2 minutes. Add the chicken and cook until the chicken is hot. Turn off the heat and stir in the lime juice, sour cream and half of the cilantro, and taste for seasoning, adding more salt or lime juice as desired. Serve hot, topped with the rest of the pepper Jack cheese, cilantro and the optional garnishes.

3 fresh Anaheim or Hatch chiles

3 fresh poblano chiles

1–2 jalapeño or serrano chiles

1 large yellow onion, peeled, cut in quarters from top to bottom

5 large cloves garlic, peeled

2 tbsp (30 ml) neutral oil (such as grapeseed), divided

Kosher salt, as needed

2 (15-oz [425-g]) cans white beans (Great Northern, navy or cannellini), drained and rinsed, divided

1 tbsp (8 g) ground cumin

1 tsp ground coriander

2 cups (480 ml) Golden Chicken Stock (page 84) or store-bought stock

2 cups (226 g) shredded pepper Jack cheese, divided

3 cups (420 g) shredded chicken (from 1 small rotisserie bird)

2 tbsp (30 ml) lime juice (from about 2 limes), plus 1 lime cut into wedges for serving

½ cup (120 ml) sour cream or Mexican crema

½ cup (8 g) roughly chopped fresh cilantro leaves, divided

OPTIONAL GARNISHES

4 scallions, white and pale-green parts only, thinly sliced

1 Hass avocado, thinly sliced

1 bunch radishes, thinly sliced

Pickled red onions

Tortilla chips

THAI COCONUT SHRIMP SOUP

If you're familiar with our blog, Nerds with Knives, you know we love a good curry, especially Thai red curry. There's just something magical in the combination of flavors: fiery curry paste, rich coconut milk, tart lime, briny fish sauce. (Just thinking about it makes our mouths water.) This soup is a riff on tom kha kai, with shrimp in place of the traditional chicken. We brine the shrimp in a mix of salt and a little bit of baking soda, which makes a big difference. The salt not only seasons the shrimp, but it helps them stay moist and tender as they cook, while the baking soda helps them retain a firm texture.

In a medium bowl, toss the shrimp with the salt and baking soda. Cover with plastic wrap and refrigerate for at least 15 minutes and up to 1 hour.

If you purchased shell-on shrimp, use the shells to make a quick stock: Heat 1 tablespoon (15 ml) of the oil in a small saucepan over medium heat. Once the oil is shimmering, add the shells (and heads, if you're lucky enough to have them), and cook, tossing often, until the shells turn pink, about 3 minutes. Pour in 2 cups (480 ml) of water and bring to a boil, then lower the heat and simmer for 7 to 10 minutes. If you don't have shells, skip making the stock and add 2 cups (480 ml) of water in the next step.

Add the remaining oil to a large Dutch oven set over medium heat. Add the garlic, shallots, ginger and lemongrass and cook, stirring often, until the shallots are soft and the garlic is fragrant, about 4 minutes. Add the curry paste and cook it, stirring often, for 2 minutes. Add the fish sauce, sugar and chicken stock. Pour the shrimp stock in through a fine-mesh sieve, pressing down on the shells until all the liquid is extracted. Bring it to a simmer, add the coconut milk and the mushrooms and cook until the mushrooms are tender, about 5 minutes. Keeping the heat at a bare simmer, add the shrimp and cook until they just turn pink and are no longer translucent in the center, 3 to 5 minutes depending on their size. Stir in the lime juice and season to taste with salt. Garnish each bowl with the scallions and cilantro.

NOTE: Different brands of curry paste vary widely in their levels of heat, so start with 2 tablespoons (32 g), taste and add more, if needed. We used Maesri brand, and 3 tablespoons (48 g) was the perfect amount for our delicate sensibilities.

---

1 lb (454 g) medium shrimp, peeled and deveined, shells reserved

1 tsp kosher salt, plus more to taste

¼ tsp baking soda

2 tbsp (30 ml) vegetable oil, divided

2 cups (480 ml) water

3 medium cloves garlic, minced or grated

2 shallots, thinly sliced into rounds

2 tbsp (12 g) grated fresh ginger or galangal

2 stalks lemongrass, cut into 2" (5-cm) sections and crushed

2–4 tbsp (32–64 g) Thai red curry paste (see Note)

¼ cup (60 ml) fish sauce

1 tbsp (14 g) palm or brown sugar

4 cups (960 ml) Golden Chicken Stock (page 84) or store-bought stock

2 (13.5-oz [400-ml]) cans coconut milk

1 cup (70 g) thinly sliced shiitake mushroom caps

3 tbsp (45 ml) fresh lime juice, plus more to taste

2 scallions, thinly sliced on the diagonal

¼ cup (4 g) cilantro leaves and tender stems

GOLDEN CHICKEN STOCK

Many of the recipes in this book call for chicken or vegetable stock, and we strongly encourage you to make your own. It goes without saying (though we'll say it) that the depth and flavor of homemade stock will be far above the quality of store-bought versions. It's also much, much cheaper to make it yourself. But one often overlooked benefit is that homemade chicken stock, unlike the packaged stuff, uses collagen-rich chicken parts—necks, backs and feet—which convert to gelatin when cooked, adding nutrition and body to any dish you care to make with it.

4–5 lbs (1.8–2.3 kg) chicken parts (necks, backs, wings, etc.)

1 lb (454 g) chicken feet (optional)

3 large carrots, cut into 1" (2.5-cm) chunks

2 large yellow onions, cut into 1" (2.5-cm) chunks

2 celery ribs, cut into 1" (2.5-cm) chunks

1 head garlic, cut in half crosswise

4 sprigs fresh thyme

1 small bunch parsley stems

2 bay leaves

2 tsp (4 g) whole black peppercorns

4 qt (4 L) cold water

Rinse all the chicken pieces thoroughly under cold running water. Add the chicken, carrots, onions, celery, garlic, thyme, parsley, bay leaves and peppercorns to a large Dutch oven and pour in the water until everything is covered by at least 2 inches (5 cm). Bring to a boil over medium-high heat, and then immediately lower the heat to a bare simmer. (Don't boil the stock or it will become cloudy.) As the stock simmers, occasionally skim off any foam as it rises to the surface. Simmer uncovered for 2 hours, and then strain the stock through a fine-mesh strainer, let it cool slightly and transfer it to airtight containers. You can refrigerate the stock for up to 5 days or freeze for up to 6 months.

NOTE: Oversized silicone ice-cube trays hold ½ cup (120 ml) of liquid in each cube. Freeze the stock in these, and then move the frozen cubes into a ziplock bag for longer storage.

Yield: 3½ to 4 quarts (3.5 to 4 L)

RICH VEGETABLE BROTH

The key to cooking really good soups and stews is starting with a deeply delicious, complex broth. This is especially important in vegetarian dishes, which don't have the luxury of collagen-rich proteins to rely on for body and flavor. This recipe is for a basic broth that can be used in any recipe, but you can adjust the flavor to suit your needs. For example, add fresh tomatoes or a little paste to use in the Baked Ribollita (page 75), or throw in some sliced ginger and scallions for a wonton broth.

1 oz (28 g) shiitake mushroom stems (you can reserve the caps for another use, such as with the Thai Coconut Shrimp Soup on page 83)

1 large yellow or red onion, cut into 1" (2.5-cm) chunks

3 large carrots, cut into 2" (5-cm) chunks

2 celery ribs, cut into 1" (2.5-cm) chunks

2–3 leeks, greens only, washed well (reserve whites for another use, such as with Potato-Leek Gratin with Thyme on page 62)

1 head garlic, split crosswise

4 sprigs fresh thyme

1 small bunch parsley stems

2 bay leaves

1 tbsp (6 g) whole black peppercorns

1 (6" [15-cm]) piece kombu (optional)

1 Parmigiano-Reggiano or Pecorino rind (optional)

4 qt (4 L) cold water

Add the mushrooms, onion, carrots, celery, leeks, garlic, thyme, parsley, bay leaves, peppercorns, kombu, if using, rind, if using, and water to a large Dutch oven. The vegetables should be covered with water by about 2 inches (5 cm). Bring this to a boil over medium-high heat, and then immediately reduce the heat to a bare simmer. Simmer, stirring occasionally, until the vegetables are fully tender and the broth is aromatic, about 1½ hours. Strain the broth through a fine-mesh sieve, let it cool and transfer it to airtight containers. You can refrigerate the broth for up to 5 days or freeze it for up to 6 months.

NOTE: Not all vegetables are suitable for making broth. Starchy tubers like potatoes and turnips will make the broth murky. Earthy beets, asparagus and radishes can overwhelm the other flavors. Zucchini and green beans become bitter when cooked for a long time. A general rule of thumb is to avoid Brassicas such as cabbage, broccoli and kale, although a little cauliflower is fine. Greens from carrots and other vegetables can be bitter, so use them sparingly. Good additions for broth are fennel, tomatoes, parsnips, scallions and mushroom caps or stems.

PASTAS, GRAINS AND PULSES

Throughout this book we make the bold claim that the Dutch oven is the one pot you need. But more than just being a flexible item of cookware, it represents comfort—a big pot filled with a warm meal to feed a whole family. And when it comes to comfort food, there's a special place in our hearts for pasta and grain dishes.

Just as the Dutch oven replaces both the sauté pan and the stockpot, it also makes the perfect pasta pot, rice cooker and baking dish. That versatility allows us to experiment and take a novel approach to familiar dishes, like our kid-friendly One-Pot Cheesy Sausage and Pasta Bake (page 103), where the sauce and pasta cook together at the same time before the whole thing gets popped in the oven until it's bubbly and melty. And our Baked Risotto with Pesto and Roasted Tomatoes (page 95), which is baked in the oven rather than simmered and stirred constantly on the stovetop. (There are better ways to cause a stir in the kitchen.)

You'll also find hearty and healthy recipes such as a dinner party–worthy Cracked Farrotto with Butternut Squash and Crispy Sage (page 100), which is a risotto made with farro instead of rice; One-Pot Crispy Chicken with Lemony Mushroom Orzo (page 96), perfect for a cozy family supper; and Crispy Tofu Grain Bowl with Charred Scallions and Kimchi-Miso Dressing (page 92).

On the subject of kimchi, we couldn't resist making Kimchi Mac and Cheese (page 99), which is best eaten standing right over the stovetop, possibly without pants on. And, for a sweet treat, we just had to include a rice pudding, and ours is sweetened with homemade Dulce de Leche (page 104) and topped with freeze-dried raspberries.

HOT-SMOKED SALMON KEDGEREE
WITH CURRY-PICKLED EGGS

The term kedgeree may not be particularly familiar to Americans, but to Brits, it brings to mind a comforting, old-fashioned breakfast dish of aromatic curried rice flecked with smoked haddock and topped with hard-boiled eggs. We've made a few changes from the traditional: Homemade hot-smoked salmon takes the place of the haddock, and we lightly pickle the eggs, cooked with soft jammy yolks, in a curry brine. Pickling the eggs will take a few days, but is absolutely worth the wait. Have it for breakfast or any time you want to feel a bit posh.

To make the curry-pickled eggs, bring a medium saucepan of water to a boil, lower the heat to a simmer and carefully add the eggs. For a runny yolk, boil for 8 minutes. For hard-boiled, cook for 10 minutes. Once cooked, plunge the eggs into a bowl of ice water. When they're cool, peel the eggs. Add the vinegar, sugar, salt, curry powder, turmeric, mustard seeds, if using, lemon peel and bay leaves to a small saucepan over medium-high heat. Bring to a simmer, stirring until the sugar and salt dissolve. Turn off the heat, add the cold water and allow the brine to cool. Place the eggs in a clean jar and pour in the brine. Place a folded paper towel on top of the liquid, which will keep the eggs fully submerged in the brine. Refrigerate for at least 3 days and up to 2 weeks.

To make the kedgeree, melt the butter in a large Dutch oven over medium heat. Add the onion and salt and cook, stirring often, until the onion is soft and translucent, 5 minutes. Add the garlic, ginger, curry powder, turmeric, coriander and cumin and cook, stirring continuously, until aromatic, about 30 seconds. Add the rice and stir until it's fully coated in the spices. Pour in the water, bring to a boil, lower the heat to a bare simmer and cover the pot. Cook for 15 minutes. Turn off the heat and fluff the rice with a fork. Stir in the fish sauce and lime juice, and then flake the fish with a fork and gently stir it in, being careful not to break it up too much. Cut three or four curry-pickled eggs in half and place them on top of the rice. Scatter over the cilantro and lime quarters and serve warm.

FOR THE CURRY-PICKLED EGGS

8 large eggs

1 cup (240 ml) white vinegar

¼ cup (50 g) sugar

1½ tsp (4 g) kosher salt

2 tbsp (12 g) mild curry powder

2 tsp (4 g) ground turmeric

1 tbsp (6 g) mustard seeds (optional)

3 strips lemon peel

2 bay leaves

1½ cups (360 ml) cold water

FOR THE KEDGEREE

3 tbsp (42 g) unsalted butter

1 medium yellow onion, finely chopped

1 tsp kosher salt

3 large cloves garlic, minced

1 tbsp (6 g) minced or grated fresh ginger

2 tsp (4 g) mild curry powder

1 tsp turmeric

½ tsp ground coriander

½ tsp ground cumin

2 cups (370 g) basmati rice

4 cups (960 ml) water

2 tbsp (30 ml) fish sauce

2 tbsp (30 ml) fresh lime juice, plus more for squeezing

1 lb (454 g) store-bought hot-smoked salmon or see instructions in Classic British Fish Pie (page 114)

½ cup (8 g) loosely packed cilantro, leaves and tender stems

1 or 2 limes, quartered, for serving

CRISPY TOFU GRAIN BOWL
WITH CHARRED SCALLIONS AND KIMCHI-MISO DRESSING

The key to a great grain bowl, like a good salad, is using a variety of flavors and textures, then tying everything together with a really excellent dressing. The heavy base of the Dutch oven makes charring the scallions and crisping the tofu a breeze. One warning: This kimchi-miso dressing is so good, it's addictive, and you'll want to slather it on everything.

To make the kimchi-miso dressing, combine the kimchi, miso, tofu, grapeseed oil, sesame oil, vinegar and sugar in a blender or food processor and puree until smooth. Season with salt, if needed. Refrigerate the dressing until ready to use. Thin it with a little water if it seems too thick. The dressing can be made 4 days ahead and stored in an airtight container in the refrigerator.

To make the tofu and grains, in a medium bowl, stir together the rice vinegar, ginger and garlic. Heat 1 tablespoon (15 ml) of the grapeseed oil in a large Dutch oven set over medium-high heat. When the oil is shimmering, add the scallions and cook, turning them occasionally with tongs, until they are soft and deeply charred, 6 to 8 minutes. (If the scallions don't fit flat in the Dutch oven, cut them in half.) Transfer the charred scallions to a cutting board and cut them into ½-inch (1.3-cm) pieces. Transfer them to the bowl with the vinegar mixture, and stir in the soy sauce. Set it aside.

Unwrap the pressed tofu and cut it into large cubes. Add the remaining grapeseed oil to the Dutch oven, set it over medium-high heat and when the oil is shimmering, add the tofu in a single layer. Cook, undisturbed, until the tofu turns very crisp and dark brown on the bottom, 3 to 4 minutes. Carefully turn and brown the other side, 4 minutes. Remove the tofu with a spatula or slotted spoon, and add it to the bowl with the scallions and carefully toss to coat. Set the bowl aside and let the tofu marinate while you cook the grains. Remove all but 1 tablespoon (15 ml) of the oil from the Dutch oven and add the farro or freekeh. With the heat on medium, toss the grains in the oil and cook, stirring often, until they smell nutty and take on a golden appearance, 3 to 4 minutes. Pour in the water and a good pinch of salt, bring it to a boil and simmer until the grains are tender, but not mushy, about 20 minutes (or check package instructions). Drain (if needed) and divide the grains into serving bowls. Add the crispy tofu, charred scallions (and any optional additions) and drizzle with the dressing.

NOTE: To drain the tofu, place it between several layers of kitchen towels, set something heavy on top (like a cast-iron skillet) and let it drain while you prep the dressing.

FOR THE KIMCHI-MISO DRESSING

¼ cup (50 g) coarsely chopped kimchi

3 tbsp (48 g) white miso

½ cup (110 g) silken tofu or mayonnaise

¼ cup (60 ml) grapeseed or other neutral oil

1 tbsp (15 ml) toasted sesame oil

1 tbsp (15 ml) rice vinegar

2 tsp (9 g) sugar or honey

Kosher salt, to taste (optional)

FOR THE TOFU AND GRAINS

2 tsp (10 ml) unseasoned rice vinegar

1 tsp grated ginger

1 tsp grated garlic

¼ cup (60 ml) grapeseed or other neutral oil, divided

12 scallions, roots trimmed

1 tbsp (15 ml) soy sauce

1 (12-oz [340-g]) block firm or extra-firm tofu, drained and pressed (see Note)

1½ cups (250 g) semi-pearled farro, freekeh or your favorite grain

3 cups (720 ml) water

Kosher salt, as needed

FOR SERVING (OPTIONAL)

Thinly sliced radishes, carrots and/or cabbage

Cubed avocado

Pickled red onions

Baby arugula or other microgreens

Limes, for squeezing

BAKED RISOTTO
WITH PESTO AND ROASTED TOMATOES

The best thing about this method of making risotto is that it takes most of the work out of the process. Instead of adding ladles of broth and constantly stirring, we add all the broth at once, pop the whole thing in the oven and stir it vigorously once the rice is mostly cooked. Easy peasy. Risotto is a wonderful base for all kinds of flavors, and here we give it a summery spin with a swirl of bright-green basil pesto and a few luscious roasted tomatoes.

If making your own pesto, add the basil, nuts, garlic and a pinch of salt and pepper to the bowl of a food processor. Pulse 10 to 15 times, scraping down the sides of the bowl with a rubber spatula, until the herbs and nuts are coarsely chopped. While the food processor is running, slowly drizzle in the olive oil, scraping down the bowl as necessary. Add the cheese and pulse it a few times to combine it with the pesto. Store the pesto in an airtight container in the refrigerator.

Preheat the oven to 375°F (190°C) and set one rack in the lower third of the oven and another in the upper third.

To make the risotto, heat 2 tablespoons (30 ml) of the olive oil in a large Dutch oven set over medium heat. When the oil is shimmering, add the onion, salt and pepper. Cook, stirring often, until the onion is translucent but not browned (about 5 minutes). Add the minced garlic and cook for 30 seconds. Add the rice and stir until each grain is coated in the oil and begins to lose its chalky look, 4 to 5 minutes. Turn the heat up to medium-high, pour in the wine and stir until it's absorbed by the rice, about 2 minutes. Add the stock and bring it to a simmer, stirring frequently. Cover the pot, place it on the lower rack in the oven and bake it for 20 minutes.

While the rice is baking, add the tomatoes and the smashed garlic to a baking dish and drizzle them with the remaining olive oil and a sprinkle of salt and pepper. Place the dish on the upper rack of the oven and cook until the tomatoes sizzle and some of them burst their skins, 12 to 15 minutes. Remove the dish from the oven and set it aside. Reserve the oil for drizzling over the rice. The tomatoes can be made up to a full day ahead and reheated for a few minutes while the rice cooks.

After the rice has baked for 20 minutes, remove the pot from the oven, take off the lid and stir the rice vigorously, making sure to scrape the bottom of the pot. Taste the rice, and if it needs more time, replace the lid, return the pot to the oven and cook until the rice is tender but with a slight firmness in the center. Take the pot out of the oven and stir in the butter and Parmigiano-Reggiano. Swirl in up to ½ cup (120 ml) of the pesto, leaving streaks of green in the white rice, and taste for seasoning. Divide the rice into serving bowls and add a few roasted garlicky tomatoes to each serving. Garnish with a few fresh basil leaves and a drizzle of the tomato-cooking olive oil.

FOR THE PESTO (IF MAKING YOUR OWN. OR FIND A GOOD STORE VERSION)

2 cups (48 g) packed fresh basil leaves or a mix of basil, parsley, chives and baby spinach

⅓ cup (50 g) lightly toasted pine nuts, walnuts or pistachios

2 medium cloves garlic, minced or grated

Kosher salt and freshly ground black pepper, to taste

½ cup (120 ml) extra-virgin olive oil

½ cup (50 g) grated Parmigiano-Reggiano or Pecorino-Romano cheese

FOR THE RISOTTO

¼ cup (60 ml) extra-virgin olive oil, divided

1 medium yellow onion, finely chopped

½ tsp kosher salt, plus more to taste

¼ tsp freshly ground black pepper, plus more to taste

7 medium cloves garlic, divided (3 minced, 4 peeled and smashed)

2 cups (390 g) carnaroli or arborio rice

¾ cup (180 ml) dry white wine

6 cups (1.4 L) Golden Chicken Stock (page 84) or store-bought stock

2 cups (300 g) cherry or Campari-style tomatoes

2 tbsp (28 g) unsalted butter

¾ cup (75 g) grated Parmigiano-Reggiano

1 small bunch basil, for serving

ONE-POT CRISPY CHICKEN
WITH LEMONY MUSHROOM ORZO

There are many reasons we make so many one-pot dinners. In a small kitchen, it keeps the clutter to a minimum, simplifies the cooking process and makes clean-up straightforward. The trick, of course, is to get everything properly cooked at the same time. This one-pot wonder combines crisp-skinned chicken baked directly on top of buttery, lemony orzo, studded with wild mushrooms, leeks and baby spinach. It's a complete (and completely delicious) dinner, made all in a single Dutch oven.

4 attached chicken legs and thighs or 8 separate pieces, bone-in and skin-on

Kosher salt and freshly ground black pepper, as needed

3 tbsp (42 g) unsalted butter, divided

¾ lb (340 g) mixed wild mushrooms or white buttons, sliced

2 medium leeks, white and pale-green parts only or a large yellow onion, chopped

3 large cloves garlic, minced

3 tsp (3 g) fresh thyme leaves or ½ tsp dried thyme

2 cups (285 g) orzo

½ cup (120 ml) dry sherry or white wine

3½ cups (830 ml) Golden Chicken Stock (page 84) or store-bought stock, divided

2 tbsp (30 ml) fresh lemon juice

2 tsp (4 g) finely grated lemon zest

3 cups (90 g) baby spinach

1 lemon, cut into wedges, for garnish

Preheat the oven to 400°F (200°C) and set a rack in the middle.

Dry the chicken well and season it generously with salt and pepper on both sides. Heat 1 tablespoon (15 g) of the butter in a large Dutch oven set over medium-high heat. Add the chicken, skin side down, in a single layer. Cook until the skin is very crisp and deep golden brown, 10 to 12 minutes. Remove the chicken to a plate and set it aside. It will not yet be fully cooked.

Add the mushrooms and leeks and cook, scraping up any brown bits from the Dutch oven and stirring occasionally, until the leeks are wilted and mushrooms are light brown, about 7 minutes. Add the garlic and thyme, season with salt and pepper and cook until the garlic is fragrant, about 1 minute. Stir in the orzo and cook, stirring often, until it starts to smell toasty, about 3 minutes. Pour in the sherry and stir until the liquid is evaporated, about 1 minute. Add 3 cups (720 ml) of the chicken stock, bring it to a simmer and cook, stirring often, for 5 minutes. Place the chicken back in the pot on top of the orzo, skin side up, and move it to the oven. Cook, uncovered, until the chicken is cooked through (it should register 165°F [75°C] on an instant-read thermometer) and the orzo is tender, 15 to 20 minutes.

Remove the pot from the oven and transfer the chicken to a platter. Stir the orzo and, if needed, stir in the remaining stock (it should be a little saucy). Stir in the lemon juice, zest and the remaining butter. Fold in the baby spinach, a handful at a time, until wilted. Taste the orzo for seasoning. Serve the chicken and orzo with lemon wedges.

KIMCHI MAC AND CHEESE

Some might say, "Don't mess with a good thing." To that, we reply, "Talk to us after you try our Kimchi Mac and Cheese," and also, "You're welcome." To temper kimchi's vinegary bite, we sauté it until the cabbage turns brown and caramelized in spots. And to make the smoothest, gooiest and tastiest mac and cheese, we combine three different cheeses: cheddar for its sharp, tangy flavor; Gruyère for its nuttiness and melting ability; and . . . yes, good old American cheese. Before you send us that angry email with the all-caps subject heading: NOT REAL CHEESE, hear us out. Nothing melts like American cheese. Except your hearts when you taste this.

1 tbsp (9 g) kosher salt

1 lb (454 g) cavatappi or other short-cut curly pasta

4 tbsp (56 g) unsalted butter

1½ cups (225 g) drained and chopped kimchi (1" [2.5-cm] pieces), plus more for garnish

3 large cloves garlic, minced or grated

5 scallions, finely sliced, green and white parts separated

¼ cup (30 g) all-purpose flour

2 tsp (3 g) mustard powder

1 cup (240 ml) whole milk

1 (12-oz [355-ml]) can evaporated milk

5 oz (142 g) American cheese slices or blocks, cut into small pieces (see Note)

¾ lb (340 g) extra-sharp cheddar cheese, grated

½ lb (227 g) Gruyère, grated

Bring a large pot of salted water to a boil and cook the pasta according to the package directions, until al dente. Reserve 1 cup (240 ml) of the pasta cooking water, drain the pasta and set it aside.

Melt the butter in a large Dutch oven over medium-high heat. Add the kimchi and cook, stirring often, until the cabbage is softened and browned in spots, 5 to 7 minutes. Add the garlic and scallion whites and cook until the garlic is fragrant, 1 minute. Add the flour and mustard powder and stir until no clumps remain, about 1 minute. Stir in the whole milk and evaporated milk, scraping the bottom of the pot to dissolve any brown bits. Bring to a boil, reduce the heat to low and simmer, stirring often until it thickens, 2 to 4 minutes. With the heat on low, add half the American cheese and stir until it's mostly melted before adding the rest. Working one large handful at a time, stir in the cheddar and the Gruyère, letting each batch melt before the next is added. Stir the cooked pasta into the cheese sauce, making sure it's fully coated. If the cheese sauce is too thick, add the reserved pasta water ¼ cup (60 ml) at a time until the desired consistency is reached. Serve immediately, sprinkled with the reserved scallion greens and topped with a little more kimchi.

NOTE: We like to use regular old Kraft singles. We don't recommend Velveeta-style cheese, which is processed even further, and we don't like the flavor it adds.

CRACKED FARROTTO
WITH BUTTERNUT SQUASH AND CRISPY SAGE

The culinary technique called risottato *refers to the act of cooking something in the style of risotto. In other words, by adding stock a little at a time, while stirring to release the starch. Farro—a protein and fiber-packed whole grain—is perfect for this treatment because it retains its toothsome texture even after a long, slow cook. Cracking half the grains by whizzing them in a blender helps release more starch during cooking and creates a creamier finished dish. We flavor the dish with sage and roasted butternut squash, and then give it an extra delicious wallop by sprinkling fried sage leaves over the top. Make plenty extra and snack on them all day.*

Preheat the oven to 425°F (220°C) and set a rack in the middle.

To make the farrotto, toss the squash with 2 tablespoons (30 ml) of the olive oil and season it well with salt and pepper. Place it on a parchment-lined baking sheet and roast for 25 to 30 minutes, turning once, until the squash is tender and the edges are browned. Remove it from the oven and set aside.

While the squash is cooking, add ¾ cup (125 g) of the farro to a blender and pulse until the farro is cracked and broken up into small pieces, 4 to 5 one-second pulses, depending on the strength of your blender.

Melt 1 tablespoon (15 g) of the butter with the remaining olive oil in a large Dutch oven set on medium heat. Add the shallots and a pinch of salt and pepper, and cook until they become soft and translucent, about 3 minutes. Add the garlic, sage and the farro (both whole and broken) and stir, coating each grain with oil. Cook until the garlic is fragrant, about 1 minute. Stir in the wine and cook until it's fully absorbed, about 2 minutes. Pour in 6 cups (1.4 L) of the stock, and bring the liquid to a full boil; stir it well, and then cover and simmer, stirring occasionally, until the farro is almost tender with a little bit of a bite to it, 35 to 45 minutes. Once the farro is at that stage, vigorously stir in the remaining stock, turn the heat off, stir in the Parmigiano-Reggiano, remaining butter and mascarpone and gently fold in the roasted squash. Season to taste with salt and pepper.

To make the crispy fried sage, heat the oil in a small skillet over medium-high heat. When the oil is shimmering, add 5 to 7 sage leaves and cook, swirling the pan, until they crisp, 5 to 10 seconds. Transfer them to a paper towel–lined plate, sprinkle with salt and repeat with the remaining leaves. Sprinkle over the farro.

FOR THE FARROTTO

1 medium butternut squash, peeled and cut into ½" (1.3-cm) cubes (about 2½ cups [350 g])

3 tbsp (45 ml) extra-virgin olive oil, divided

Kosher salt and freshly ground black pepper, as needed

1½ cups (250 g) semi-pearled farro, divided

3 tbsp (42 g) unsalted butter, divided

4 medium shallots or 1 medium yellow onion, finely chopped (about 1 cup [160 g])

3 large cloves garlic, minced

7 sage leaves, minced, plus more for fried sage garnish

¾ cup (180 ml) dry white wine or dry vermouth

7 cups (1.7 L) Golden Chicken Stock (page 84), Rich Vegetable Broth (page 87) or store-bought versions of either, divided

¼ cup (25 g) grated Parmigiano-Reggiano

2 tbsp (30 g) mascarpone cheese

FOR THE CRISPY SAGE

2–3 tbsp (30–45 ml) extra-virgin olive oil

10 or more sage leaves

Kosher salt, to taste

ONE-POT CHEESY SAUSAGE AND PASTA BAKE

If you've ever been to a party that had a kids' food table and a grown-up food table, you probably noticed that everyone, of all ages, wants to eat the kid food. Us, too. This recipe is a rich marriage of meaty, cheesy flavors in an Italian-style family dish that everyone can fall in love with. You can use pork or turkey sausage, or leave the meat (and the anchovies) out for a vegetarian version. One of the cool things about this recipe is that it is truly one-pot: The pasta cooks right in the sauce, and the whole thing bakes in the Dutch oven, al forno style.

Preheat the oven to 375°F (190°C) and set a rack in the middle.

Heat the olive oil in a large Dutch oven over medium-high heat. Add the sausage and cook, breaking it up into crumbles with a wooden spoon, until browned and just cooked through, about 5 minutes. Add the onion along with a good pinch of salt and pepper, and cook, stirring often, until the onion begins to soften, about 5 minutes. Stir in the garlic, anchovies and red pepper flakes, and cook, stirring frequently, until fragrant, about 1 minute. Add the wine and tomatoes and bring to a boil. Lower the heat and simmer for 10 minutes. Stir in the pasta, water and 1 teaspoon of kosher salt. Bring to a boil, cover, reduce the heat to a simmer and cook until the pasta is al dente, 3 minutes shy of the package directions. Remove it from the heat and stir in ½ cup (50 g) of the Parmigiano-Reggiano until it melts. Then stir in ½ cup (56 g) of the mozzarella and dot the top with the remaining cheeses. Place the pot in the oven, uncovered, and bake until the pasta is fully cooked and the cheese on top is bubbly and brown in spots, about 10 minutes. Sprinkle with basil and serve hot.

2 tbsp (30 ml) extra-virgin olive oil

1½ lbs (680 g) pork or turkey Italian sausage, casings removed

1 large yellow onion, diced

1 tsp kosher salt, plus more as needed

Freshly ground black pepper, as needed

5 large cloves garlic, minced

3 anchovy filets, minced

½ tsp crushed red pepper flakes, plus more to taste

1 cup (240 ml) dry red wine

1 (28-oz [794-g]) can crushed tomatoes

1 lb (454 g) tofette or other short-cut pasta

2 cups (480 ml) water

¾ cup (75 g) grated Parmigiano-Reggiano or Pecorino cheese, divided

¾ lb (340 g) packaged mozzarella, cut into ½" (1.3-cm) cubes, divided

½ cup (12 g) roughly torn basil leaves

DULCE DE LECHE RICE PUDDING

Rice pudding is a classic homey dessert, but like almost anything, it can be made even more delicious with the addition of homemade dulce de leche. Using risotto rice (we like carnaroli) ensures the creamiest texture. The added dulce de leche adds a gorgeous caramel complexity, a topping of salty pistachios adds crunch and a few berries give a pop of bright color and tartness.

1 (14-oz [414-ml]) can sweetened condensed milk or store-bought dulce de leche

3½ cups (840 ml) whole milk

1 cup (240 ml) half-and-half

1 cup (200 g) uncooked carnaroli or arborio rice

1 large cinnamon stick, broken in half

¼ tsp kosher salt

2 large egg yolks, room temperature

1 tsp vanilla extract or paste

1 tbsp (15 ml) dark rum

¼ cup (30 g) roughly chopped salted pistachios, for serving (optional)

½ cup (75 g) fresh, frozen or freeze-dried berries, for serving (optional)

To make the dulce de leche, remove the paper label from the can of condensed milk and place the unopened can on its side in your Dutch oven. Fill the pot with cool water, making sure the water level is at least 2 inches (5 cm) above the can. Turn the heat on high and bring it to a boil. Reduce the heat to a simmer, cover and cook for 2½ hours. Check the water level every 30 minutes to ensure the can remains submerged, adding boiling water as needed. Remove the can from the water using a pair of tongs, and set it on a wire rack to cool fully before opening. Do not attempt to open the can while it's still hot because the pressure may cause hot caramel to spray out. The unopened can of dulce de leche can be stored at room temperature for up to 3 months. Once opened, transfer it to an airtight container and refrigerate it for up to 3 weeks.

To make the rice pudding, add the milk, half-and-half, rice, cinnamon stick and salt to a medium or large Dutch oven. Turn the heat to medium-high and bring it to a boil. Reduce the heat to low and simmer, stirring often, until the rice is tender, about 20 minutes. In a medium mixing bowl, whisk together the egg yolks and the dulce de leche until they are fully combined. While whisking continuously, slowly drizzle about 1 cup (185 g) of the hot rice mixture into the egg yolk–caramel mixture until they're fully combined. Stir the warmed egg mixture back into the rice, and cook over low heat, stirring often, until the rice becomes thick and creamy, about 10 minutes. If the pudding is too thick, stir in water or milk, a few tablespoons (30 ml) at a time, until the texture is as you like it. Remove the cinnamon stick and stir in the vanilla and rum. Serve the rice pudding hot or at room temperature with a topping of chopped pistachios and a few berries, if desired.

SWEET AND SAVORY
PIES AND CRUMBLES

In our minds, there's very little you can bring to the center of a dinner table that will elicit as much excitement as a freshly baked pie.

The United States, the unchallenged champion of the sweet pie, has been somewhat slow to embrace savory versions, so we've imported a couple from Matt's native land: a Classic British Fish Pie (page 114), which is a creamy concoction filled with cod, shrimp and smoked salmon, and Our Very Favorite Shepherd's Pie (page 109), which is a combined version of the beloved shepherd's and cottage pies. Even our chicken pot pie gets a fun twist: Under the buttery puff pastry top lies a delicious aromatic curry, with fragrant spices and a creamy tomato gravy (see Chicken Makhani Curry Pot Pie on page 113). There's also Ruffled Spanakopita Pie (page 110) as a tribute to Astoria, Queens, where we first met.

For sweet pies, we turn to American history to inspire us, with an Apple-Caramel Pandowdy (page 119) that would be right at home in a Revolutionary kitchen, as well as a Blackberry-Ginger Slump with Rosemary Dumplings (page 120) and a Plum, Raspberry and Almond Crumble (page 116).

For all these recipes, you can use whatever size Dutch oven you have, but a shallow oven (braiser-style), or a smaller 2- to 3-quart (2- to 3-L) oven are ideal for this kind of cooking. (You won't need the lid for any of these recipes.) You can also prepare the ingredients in the Dutch oven and transfer them for baking into a smaller baking dish or individual cocottes.

If your goal is to wow your dinner guests, there's something in this chapter for you, whether it's topped with creamy mashed potatoes, golden brown puff pastry or sweet almond streusel. Easy as pie.

OUR VERY FAVORITE SHEPHERD'S PIE

Shepherd's pie is made with lamb, while cottage pie uses beef. We like the flavor of a mix of both. Our version is an absolute umami bomb, combining Worcestershire sauce, anchovies, tomato paste, Marmite brand yeast extract (not so familiar in the U.S., but it is catching on!) and red wine to make the filling ultra-savory.

To make the mashed potatoes, add the potatoes to a colander and rinse them under cold water until the water runs clear, about 1 minute. Transfer them to a large saucepan and add enough cold water to cover them by at least 2 inches (5 cm). Add the salt and bring the water to a boil over high heat, and then reduce the heat to a simmer and cook until a knife easily pierces the potatoes, 10 to 15 minutes. Drain the potatoes in the colander and rinse them again with hot running water for 30 seconds. Drain well, transfer to a large bowl and mash them with the butter and half-and-half until smooth. Taste for seasoning and add salt and pepper as desired. Stir in the yolk until well combined. Press plastic wrap directly against the surface of the potatoes to prevent a skin from forming, and set the bowl aside.

To make the filling, in a large bowl, add the beef, lamb, salt, baking soda and water. Mix with your hands until it's evenly combined. Cover with plastic wrap and let the mixture sit on the counter for 20 minutes. Heat the oil in a large Dutch oven over high heat. When the oil is shimmering, add the ground meat and cook, stirring occasionally, until it's well browned, 8 to 10 minutes. If the meat releases a lot of fat, use a spoon to ladle most of it out, leaving just 2 tablespoons (30 ml) in the pot. Add the onions, carrots and celery and cook, stirring and scraping the bottom of the pot, until the vegetables begin to soften slightly, about 4 minutes. Add the garlic, anchovies and the tomato paste and stir for 1 minute. Sprinkle the flour in and stir until it's well incorporated, about 2 minutes. Stir in the red wine, chicken stock, rosemary, thyme, Worcestershire and Marmite, if using. Bring the liquid to a simmer, and then reduce the heat to low and simmer until the sauce is reduced and thick, about 20 minutes. Stir in the peas and season to taste with salt and pepper.

Heat the oven to 425°F (220°C) and set a rack in the middle.

At this point, you can either finish the dish in your Dutch oven or transfer the filling to a 9 x 13–inch (23 x 33–cm) baking dish. Either way, dollop spoonfuls of the mashed potatoes on top, and use a spatula to gently spread them out so they cover the meat completely. Smooth out the top, and then use a fork to make furrows over the surface. Set the Dutch oven or baking dish on top of a foil-lined baking tray (to catch any drips) and transfer to the oven. Bake until the top is browned and the pie is fully heated through, 20 to 25 minutes. If you want a darker top, you can set it under the broiler for 1 to 2 minutes. Let the pie sit for at least 15 minutes before serving. The pie can be assembled, covered with plastic wrap and refrigerated for up to 2 days. Reheat in a 350°F (180°C) oven for 35 to 40 minutes.

FOR THE MASHED POTATOES

3½ lbs (1.6 kg) russet potatoes (about 4 large), peeled and cut into 1" (2.5-cm) cubes

2 tbsp (16 g) kosher salt, plus more to taste

6 tbsp (84 g) unsalted butter, cubed

½ cup (120 ml) half-and-half

Freshly ground black pepper, to taste

1 egg yolk

FOR THE FILLING

1¼ lbs (568 g) 85 percent lean ground beef

1¼ lbs (568 g) ground lamb

2 tsp (6 g) kosher salt, plus more as needed

¾ tsp baking soda

1 tbsp (15 ml) cold water

2 tbsp (30 ml) neutral oil

2 large yellow onions, finely chopped

3 medium carrots, peeled and finely chopped

2 celery ribs, finely chopped

4 large cloves garlic, minced

2 anchovy filets, minced

2 tbsp (32 g) tomato paste

2 tbsp (16 g) all-purpose flour

1 cup (240 ml) dry red wine

1 cup (240 ml) Golden Chicken Stock (page 84) or store-bought stock

2 tsp (1 g) chopped rosemary leaves

2 tsp (1 g) chopped thyme leaves

1 tbsp (15 ml) Worcestershire sauce

1 tsp Marmite (optional)

8 oz (227 g) frozen peas

Freshly ground black pepper, to taste

RUFFLED SPANAKOPITA PIE

When we lived in Astoria in the New York borough of Queens, every Greek food market made their own excellent spanakopita, which is a spinach and feta pie layered in phyllo pastry. Our version takes an easy route with frozen spinach, but perks up the flavor with a full cup of fresh herbs. Making this in the Dutch oven gives you only one pot to clean, and keeping the extra-crispy ruffled phyllo only on the top layer means that you won't have to worry about the pie having a soggy bottom. (No one likes a soggy bottom.)

4 (10-oz [283-g]) packages frozen chopped spinach, thawed

¼ cup (60 ml) extra-virgin olive oil

2 large leeks, white and pale-green parts only, thinly sliced

1½ tsp (4 g) kosher salt

½ tsp freshly ground black pepper

5 scallions, white and pale-green parts only, sliced

4 large cloves garlic, grated or minced

¼ cup (43 g) uncooked couscous

2 large eggs

½ cup (123 g) ricotta cheese

1 cup (50 g) packed chopped fresh tender herbs (see Note)

2 tsp (4 g) finely grated lemon zest

12 oz (340 g) Greek or French feta, crumbled in large curds

12 (9 x 14" [23 x 36–cm]) sheets frozen phyllo pastry, thawed

5 tbsp (75 ml) melted salted butter, cooled

Preheat the oven to 350°F (180°C) and place a rack in the middle.

Squeeze the excess water out of the thawed spinach by placing it in the center of a clean kitchen towel and twisting it over the sink until most of the liquid comes out. It doesn't need to be bone-dry, just not sopping wet. Transfer the spinach to a large bowl and use a fork to break up the clumps.

Heat the oil in a large Dutch oven set over medium heat. Add the leeks, salt and pepper, and cook, stirring, until the leeks just begin to soften, about 5 minutes. Add the scallions and garlic, and cook until the vegetables are tender, 5 minutes. Turn off the heat and scrape the mixture into the bowl with the spinach. Add the couscous and stir.

In a medium bowl, whisk the eggs, and then stir in the ricotta, chopped herbs and lemon zest and mix it together. Pour the egg mixture into the spinach and mix it well. Gently fold in the feta, being careful not to break up all the curds. Transfer the mixture back into the Dutch oven and spread it into an even layer.

Place the phyllo sheets on the counter under a slightly damp kitchen towel. Lay 1 sheet of phyllo on a work surface and brush it generously with melted butter on one side, and then scrunch up the sheet and place it on top of the spinach mixture in the pot—the more folds, the better. Repeat with the remaining phyllo, layering the sheets until the spinach is completely covered. Drizzle any remaining butter over the top of the dough. Using a sharp knife or a skewer, poke several holes straight down through the dough. Bake the pie until the phyllo is golden brown and crisp, 45 to 50 minutes. Let it cool in the pan for at least 20 minutes before serving.

NOTE: We use a mix of what grows best in our garden—basil, parsley, chives and dill—but you can use whatever tender herbs you like. Avoid woody herbs like thyme and rosemary, as their flavor would be too strong here.

CHICKEN MAKHANI CURRY POT PIE

The classic American chicken pot pie gets an Indian twist and we're super psyched about it. After marinating in yogurt and spices, the chicken gets browned and then simmered in a mildly spiced tomato and onion–based curry sauce. While absolutely delicious on its own, we add our favorite pot pie vegetables (peas and pearl onions), top it with a puff pastry crust and bake it until it turns deep golden brown.

Preheat the oven to 425°F (220°C) and set a rack in the middle.

To make the chicken marinade, in a large bowl, add the chicken, salt, yogurt, garam masala, turmeric, cumin, chili flakes, ginger and garlic. Toss well and let it marinate for 30 minutes at room temperature or refrigerate it for up to 1 day.

To make the Makhani sauce, heat the oil in a large Dutch oven set over medium-high heat. When the oil is shimmering, add the chicken, working in two or three batches as needed so as not to crowd the pot. Sear until browned and charred in spots but not fully cooked, about 3 minutes per side. Remove the chicken to a plate and set it aside.

Turn the heat down to medium, melt the ghee in the pot and add the onion and salt. Cook, stirring occasionally, until the onion softens and begins to turn golden brown, 10 to 12 minutes. If the bottom of the pot threatens to burn, add 1 to 2 tablespoons (15 to 30 ml) of water and scrape up the brown bits that form on the bottom of the pot. Add the ginger and garlic and sauté, stirring constantly, until fragrant, about 1 minute. Add the garam masala, cumin, coriander and flour. Cook, stirring constantly, until the onion is coated in the spices and the flour. Add the tomatoes and their juices plus the water and bring to a boil. Reduce the heat to maintain a gentle simmer. Cook, stirring and scraping the bottom of the pot occasionally, until the liquid has reduced and turned a darker reddish brown, about 30 minutes.

When the sauce is ready, turn off the heat and with an immersion blender, blend the sauce until it becomes completely smooth, about 2 minutes. Stir in the crème fraîche, kasuri methi, if using, peas and pearl onions. Add the chicken, along with any accumulated juices, back into the pot and set it aside. Roll out the puff pastry on a lightly floured surface until it's large enough to cover the pot with an overhang of about 1 inch (2.5 cm) on all sides. Drape the pastry over the pot and press firmly around the edges with your fingers or with the tines of a fork to make it adhere. Lightly brush the pastry with the egg wash and cut two to three small slits in the center to allow steam to escape. Bake the pot pie until the crust is puffed and light golden brown, about 20 minutes, then reduce the oven temperature to 350°F (180°C) and continue to bake until the filling is bubbling around the edges and the crust is deep brown, 20 to 25 minutes. Let it sit for 10 minutes before serving. Spoon a serving onto a plate and sprinkle it with cilantro.

FOR THE CHICKEN MARINADE

4 lbs (1.8 kg) boneless, skinless chicken thighs or breasts, cut into 1" (2.5-cm) pieces

2 tsp (6 g) kosher salt

½ cup (120 ml) Greek yogurt

1 tbsp (6 g) garam masala

1 tsp turmeric

1 tsp ground cumin

1 tsp Aleppo-style chili flakes

1 tbsp (6 g) peeled and finely grated fresh ginger

3 large cloves garlic, grated or minced

FOR THE MAKHANI SAUCE

2 tbsp (30 ml) grapeseed oil or other neutral oil

1 tbsp (15 g) ghee or unsalted butter

1 large Spanish onion, diced

2 tsp (6 g) kosher salt

1 tbsp (6 g) peeled and grated or finely chopped fresh ginger

4 medium cloves garlic, smashed and roughly chopped

1 tbsp (6 g) garam masala

1½ tsp (3 g) ground cumin

1 tsp (3 g) ground coriander

3 tbsp (24 g) all-purpose flour

3 (15-oz [425-g]) cans diced fire-roasted tomatoes

½ cup (120 ml) water

1 cup (240 ml) crème fraîche or heavy cream

2 tsp (1 g) kasuri methi (fenugreek leaves) (optional)

1 (13-oz [370-g]) bag frozen peas, thawed and drained

1 (13-oz [370-g]) bag frozen pearl onions, thawed and drained

1 sheet frozen puff pastry, defrosted

1 large egg, beaten with 1 tsp water

Cilantro, for garnish

CLASSIC BRITISH FISH PIE

In Matt's homeland of Britain, the coast was never too far away, there was always fresh seafood and one of the best uses of good fish was to make a fish pie. This version combines three types of seafood covered with a fluffy mashed potato topping. You can simplify the process and buy hot-smoked salmon from your local market, but our recommendation is to use a grill or smoker to smoke your own salmon. It's much cheaper and easier than you might think. This combination of super-fresh seafood and a rich sauce is something you'll want to reel in.

To make the smoked salmon, combine the sugar, salt, pepper, mustard powder and lemon zest in a small bowl. Place the salmon, skin side down, in a glass dish. Spread the mixture evenly on top of the salmon. Cover the dish with plastic wrap and refrigerate for at least 4 hours or up to 12 hours. If you're using wood chips, soak them in water for at least 1½ hours before you plan to smoke the fish. Light a chimney full of charcoal. When all the charcoal is lit and covered with gray ash, pour out and arrange the coals on one side of the charcoal grate. Sprinkle half the soaked wood chips over the hot coals. You can also use a smoker box or a foil packet with holes punched in it. On the empty side of the grill, place the foil pan and pour in 1 cup (240 ml) of water. Place the cooking grate on the grill. Make sure the top and bottom vents are open about one-quarter of the way. Wipe most of the sugar mixture off the salmon and place the fish, skin side down, on the cooler side of the grill directly over the foil pan. Close the lid on the grill and smoke the salmon for about 20 minutes. The interior of the fish should reach 125°F (52°C) on an instant thermometer and feel just firm to the touch. Allow the salmon to rest off the heat for at least 20 minutes and once it's cool, remove the skin and any bones, and flake into medium 1-inch (2.5-cm) pieces.

To make the potatoes, transfer the cubed potatoes to a bowl of cold water to rinse. In your Dutch oven, bring the water to a boil over high heat. Add the potatoes and cook until completely tender, about 15 minutes. Drain in a colander and rinse them under hot running water for 30 seconds to wash away the excess starch. Use a ricer or hand masher to mash the potatoes in a bowl, and then add the milk and butter and fold gently with a rubber spatula to combine. Season to taste with salt and pepper. Transfer the potatoes to a large bowl and wash out the Dutch oven for the next step.

Heat the oven to 375°F (190°C) and arrange a rack in the middle.

NOTE: If you don't want to smoke your own salmon, you can buy ½ lb (227 g) hot-smoked salmon.

FOR THE SMOKED SALMON

½ cup (100 g) sugar

1 tbsp (8 g) kosher salt

2 tsp (4 g) coarsely ground black pepper

2 tsp (6 g) mustard powder

2 tsp (4 g) grated lemon zest

½ lb (227 g) salmon fillets, skin on

1 large, flat disposable foil pan

1 cup (240 ml) water

FOR THE MASHED POTATOES

2 lbs (908 g) Idaho or russet potatoes, peeled and cut into 1–2" (2.5–5-cm) cubes

4 qt (4 L) water

½ cup (120 ml) whole milk

6 tbsp (84 g) unsalted butter

Coarse kosher salt and freshly ground black pepper, to taste

To make the filling, in a medium bowl, toss the shrimp with the salt and baking soda. Place it in the fridge for 15 minutes or up to 1 hour. When ready, cut the shrimp into large chunks if they're extra-large or jumbo.

In the Dutch oven over medium heat, melt 4 tablespoons (60 g) of the butter. Add the leeks and cook until they're soft but not brown, about 5 minutes. Stir in the flour and cook for 2 minutes. Slowly add the wine, milk and cream, stirring well. Bring the sauce to a simmer and cook for 5 minutes. Stir in the parsley, chives and anchovies. Remove from the heat and season to taste with salt and pepper. Gently stir in the smoked salmon, white fish and shrimp.

Top the fish with dollops of mashed potatoes, and then use a spatula to spread them into an even layer over the entire top of the dish. (You can use the back of a large spoon to create a wavy texture on the potatoes, if you like.) Sprinkle over the panko breadcrumbs and dot the top with the remaining butter. Place the Dutch oven on a baking tray and place it in the oven on the center rack. Bake until bubbly and the top is golden brown, 30 to 40 minutes.

FOR THE FILLING

½ lb (227 g) large shrimp, peeled and deveined

½ tsp coarse kosher salt, plus more to taste

⅛ tsp baking soda

6 tbsp (84 g) unsalted butter, divided

2 medium leeks, white and pale-green parts only, washed and finely chopped

⅓ cup (42 g) all-purpose flour

½ cup (120 ml) dry white wine

1 cup (240 ml) whole milk

1 cup (240 ml) heavy cream

¼ cup (15 g) chopped parsley

3 tbsp (10 g) minced chives

2 anchovy filets, finely chopped

Freshly ground black pepper, to taste

1 lb (454 g) firm white fish (cod, halibut, haddock or hake), skinned, deboned and cut into 1½" (4-cm) chunks

½ cup (28 g) panko breadcrumbs

PLUM, RASPBERRY AND ALMOND CRUMBLE

Is there anything better than biting into a piece of perfectly ripe summer fruit? Yes! Biting into perfectly ripe summer fruit that's been baked with a crispy, buttery streusel topping. Any good, in-season fruit, like peaches or nectarines, will work well in a crumble, but we really love using plums for their incredible color and sweet-tart flavor. Our raspberry bush just happened to be gloriously abundant as we were putting this book together, and we couldn't resist throwing some berries into the mix: The pops of bright berry tartness go perfectly with the jammy, luscious plums.

Heat the oven to 350°F (180°C) and set a rack in the middle.

To make the crumble topping, add the flour, oats, sugar, salt, cinnamon and ginger to a medium bowl and stir to combine. Add the butter and using a fork or your fingers, rub it into the flour mix until a coarse meal forms. Add the almonds and mix them in, allowing some slices to break up and some to remain whole. Cover the bowl with plastic wrap and refrigerate until you're ready to use it. The crumble topping can be prepared up to 1 day ahead.

To make the filling, add the plums, raspberries, sugar, salt, flour, brandy, if using, and vanilla to a medium or large Dutch oven and gently toss everything together. Remove the crumble topping from the refrigerator and use your hands to squeeze bits of the dough into soft clumps, scattering them over the fruit. Bake until the plums soften and bubble around the edges and the topping browns, 45 minutes to 1 hour. Allow it to cool for at least 15 minutes before serving with ice cream, crème fraîche, mascarpone or whipped cream.

NOTE: Plums can vary greatly in sweetness, depending on variety and season. Taste one of your plums; if your mouth puckers, use 5 to 6 tablespoons (65 to 75 g) of the sugar instead of 4 tablespoons (50 g).

FOR THE CRUMBLE TOPPING

¾ cup (94 g) all-purpose flour

¾ cup (68 g) old-fashioned rolled oats

¾ cup (168 g) turbinado or light brown sugar

2 tsp (6 g) kosher salt

½ tsp ground cinnamon

¼ tsp ground ginger

10 tbsp (140 g) very cold unsalted butter, cut into small cubes

1 cup (108 g) sliced almonds

FOR THE FILLING

4 lbs (1.8 kg) plums or other stone fruit, halved, pitted and cut into wedges

1 cup (120 g) fresh or frozen raspberries

4–6 tbsp (50–75 g) sugar (see Note)

½ tsp kosher salt

¼ cup (30 g) all-purpose flour

3 tbsp (45 ml) brandy or rum (optional)

2 tsp (10 ml) vanilla paste or extract

FOR SERVING

Ice cream, crème fraîche, mascarpone or whipped cream

APPLE-CARAMEL PANDOWDY

We live in New York's Hudson Valley, which is prime apple country. It's practically a requirement to don a cozy sweater and skip through an orchard at the first sign of fall. The pandowdy is a classic American dessert (it was First Lady Abigail Adams' favorite!). The name comes from the dowdy appearance of the haphazardly cut pieces of dough as well as the brown bits that form when the juices bubble up and caramelize the crust. The flavor though . . . that's anything but frumpy.

To make the dough, in a food processor, pulse the flour, sugar and salt until combined. Add the butter and sour cream and pulse until the butter is the size of peas, about 10 one-second pulses. Drizzle in the ice water and pulse until evenly moistened crumbs form. Turn the dough out onto a large piece of plastic wrap, form it into a ball and press it into a round disk about 1 inch (2.5 cm) thick. Cover the dough with the plastic wrap and refrigerate for at least 1 hour.

Preheat the oven to 375°F (190°C) and set a rack in the middle.

To make the filling, melt the butter in a shallow, medium-sized Dutch oven set over medium heat. Once the butter melts, swirl the pan constantly until the butter smells nutty and golden-brown bits form at the bottom of the pan (this is easier to see in a light-colored pot), 5 to 7 minutes. Add the brown sugar, cinnamon, nutmeg and salt and cook, stirring constantly, until the sugar melts and begins to bubble. Add the apples and toss to coat them in the sugar. Cover and cook, stirring occasionally, until the apples begin to soften and release some of their juice, 10 to 15 minutes. In a small bowl or measuring cup, whisk together the cider, rum, flour, lemon juice, lemon zest and vanilla until no lumps of flour remain. Pour it into the apple mixture, stirring to combine. Bring to a simmer and cook, uncovered, stirring occasionally, until the sauce is thickened, about 3 minutes. Remove the pot from the heat, and use a spoon to lightly press the apples into an even layer.

To make the topping, in a small bowl, combine the sugar and cinnamon. On a lightly floured surface, roll out the dough to about ⅛ inch (3 mm) thick, and cut it into 2-inch (5-cm) circles or squares. Traditionally, the pieces can be pretty haphazard, but you can use a biscuit cutter if you prefer more even shapes. Arrange the pieces of dough in an overlapping patchwork pattern over the apples, leaving a few openings for steam to escape. Brush the dough with the egg and sprinkle with the cinnamon sugar. Bake until the crust is slightly puffed and beginning to brown, about 25 minutes. Remove from the oven, and using the back of a large spoon, press down on the crust in various places, until some of the juice bubbles up over the top of the dough. Make sure all the apples are submerged and return the pot to the oven. Continue to bake until the crust is golden brown and the juices are bubbling, about 15 minutes. Let the pandowdy cool for at least 20 minutes, and then serve with vanilla ice cream, if using, spooning extra sauce over the top.

FOR THE DOUGH

1¼ cups (156 g) all-purpose flour, plus more for dusting

1 tbsp (13 g) sugar

½ tsp kosher salt

8 tbsp (112 g) very cold unsalted butter, cut into small cubes

1 tbsp (15 ml) sour cream or Greek yogurt, cold

¼ cup (60 ml) ice-cold water

FOR THE FILLING

6 tbsp (84 g) unsalted butter

⅔ cup (145 g) packed light brown sugar

2 tsp (7 g) ground cinnamon

¼ tsp nutmeg

½ tsp kosher salt

4 lbs (1.8 kg) apples (a mix of Granny Smith, Honeycrisp, Pink Lady or Braeburn is recommended), peeled, cored and cut into ½" (1.3-cm) wedges

¾ cup (180 ml) apple cider

2 tbsp (30 ml) dark rum

3 tbsp (24 g) all-purpose flour

2 tsp (10 ml) lemon juice

1 tsp finely grated lemon zest

1 tbsp (15 ml) vanilla extract or paste

FOR THE TOPPING

1 tbsp (13 g) granulated or turbinado sugar

½ tsp ground cinnamon

1 large egg, lightly beaten

FOR SERVING

1 qt (1 L) vanilla ice cream (optional)

BLACKBERRY-GINGER SLUMP
WITH ROSEMARY DUMPLINGS

While grunts, slumps, buckles and betties all sound like adorably old-fashioned insults, they actually belong to the same family of fruit desserts as cobblers, crisps and crumbles. So what exactly is a slump? We'll clear that right up for you: A slump is a grunt that is baked in the oven instead of simmered on the stovetop. Capisce? No? Fair enough. All you really need to know is that the combination of sweet blackberries and spicy ginger is a winner, especially topped with dumplings perfumed with just a hint of rosemary. The fact that they slump down into the softened fruit is all part of the vintage charm.

To make the dumplings, whisk together the flour, sugar, salt, baking powder and baking soda in a large bowl. Cut the butter up into small pieces and add it in. Using your hands, a pastry cutter or a fork, work the butter into the flour mixture until about half of it looks like coarse meal and the rest is left in pea-sized pieces. Add the buttermilk and rosemary and stir until the flour is just moistened, while handling the dough as little as possible. Turn it out onto a sheet of plastic wrap, press it into a loose disk shape, cover it completely and refrigerate it while you prepare the filling.

Preheat the oven to 400°F (200°C) and set a rack in the middle.

To make the filling, combine the blackberries, candied ginger, sugar, lemon juice, zest and water into a Dutch oven and place over medium heat. Bring the mixture to a simmer, decrease the heat to medium-low and cook, stirring occasionally, until the sugar melts and the berries release some of their juices, 3 to 5 minutes. Take the dough out of the refrigerator and, using your hands or a spoon, tear off roughly 2-inch (5-cm) chunks and evenly distribute them over the top of the fruit. Sprinkle the turbinado sugar evenly over the top, if using. Place the pot in the oven and bake for 20 to 25 minutes, or until the top turns light golden brown. Remove the pot from the oven and allow it to cool for 15 minutes before serving. Serve warm with a scoop of vanilla ice cream, a dollop of whipped cream or a drizzle of clotted cream.

FOR THE DUMPLINGS

2 cups (250 g) all-purpose flour

2 tbsp (26 g) sugar

½ tsp kosher salt

2 tsp (8 g) baking powder

½ tsp baking soda

5 tbsp (70 g) very cold unsalted butter

1 cup (240 ml) buttermilk, kefir or plain yogurt

2 tsp (3 g) minced fresh rosemary

FOR THE FILLING

6 cups (900 g) fresh or frozen blackberries or other berries

3 tbsp (18 g) finely chopped candied ginger

1 cup (200 g) sugar (use a little less if your blackberries are unusually sweet)

1 tsp lemon juice

1 tsp lemon zest

½ cup (120 ml) water

FOR SERVING

½–1 tbsp (7–13 g) turbinado sugar (optional)

Vanilla ice cream, whipped cream or clotted cream

REALLY SIMPLE BREADS

Jim Lahey at the Sullivan Street Bakery in New York originally popularized a method for slow-proofed, no-knead bread, ideally baked in a Dutch oven, which we gratefully adopted for this book. You can think of the Dutch oven as a kiln fired with heat. Its heavy, sealed lid traps the steam that develops moist convection in the pot as the loaf begins to rise. (We sometimes add a few ice cubes with the dough to encourage this process.)

Home bread baking is a seductive and rewarding activity that uses inexpensive ingredients and demands nothing of you but time. We chose some recipes that best made use of the Dutch oven and employed some of our favorite ingredients. We start with the Basic Dutch Oven No-Knead Bread (page 125), which produces a general-purpose loaf perfect for slathering with butter; we also include recipes for a No-Knead Cheddar-Jalapeño Bread (page 126), a variation of the basic loaf that's ideal for a grilled-cheese sandwich; an Olive and Roasted Garlic Pull-Apart Focaccia (page 129), which we love to serve as an appetizer; and a Beer, Honey and Sesame Seed Bread (page 130), which can be made in a single day. We hope you enjoy the process—and the breads—as much as we do.

Besides a Dutch oven, the second most helpful tool for baking bread at home is a kitchen scale. We list dry ingredient amounts in this chapter by weight, which always gives you more accurate and consistent results than volumetric (cup) measurements.

Note: These recipes ask you to put your Dutch ovens into an oven at very high temperatures. Make sure that the vessel you use is temperature safe. Phenolic (black plastic) lid knobs for older Le Creuset Dutch ovens, for example, are not safe above 375°F (190°C), but they can be swapped out for newer phenolic or stainless-steel versions. Most ceramic Dutch ovens are not suitable for high-temperature pre-heating, so for this chapter we strongly recommend ovens with a cast-iron core, whether enameled or not.

BASIC DUTCH OVEN NO-KNEAD BREAD

This method of baking bread without kneading uses a long proofing time to do the work of developing the gluten. We like to do the second rise on a sheet of lightly floured parchment, which makes it very easy to transfer the dough into the preheated pot and to remove it when the bread is ready. This process results in a loaf with a beautiful, deep brown crust and an airy crumb. The hardest part is leaving it alone to cool: You'll want to slice it immediately.

400 g (3¼ cups) all-purpose flour, plus additional for dusting work surface

1 g (¼ tsp) instant yeast

12 g (2 tsp) fine sea salt

Just less than 1½ cups (345 ml) lukewarm water (65–72°F [18–22°C])

Wheat bran, cornmeal or additional flour for dusting (see Note)

2–3 ice cubes

NOTE: Wheat bran or cornmeal are good options for dusting and add texture and flavor to the crust.

In a large bowl, stir together the flour, yeast and salt. Add the water, and using your fingers or a wooden spoon, stir until it just comes together. The dough will be craggy and sticky. Cover the bowl with plastic wrap and let it sit at room temperature (about 72°F [22°C]), out of direct sunlight, until the surface is dotted with bubbles and the dough has more than doubled in size. This will take between 12 and (even better) 18 hours. The slower the rise, the more complex the flavor will be. If you want to slow the rise down to suit your baking schedule, you can refrigerate the dough until you're ready for the second rise.

Once the first rise is complete, generously sprinkle a work surface with flour. Use a bowl scraper or rubber spatula to coax the dough out of the bowl. It will be quite loose and sticky, but do not add more flour. Use lightly floured hands or a bowl scraper to pull the corners of the dough in toward the center, roughly making a ball. Nudge and tuck in the edges to make it round.

Place a large piece of parchment paper next to the dough and generously dust it with wheat bran, cornmeal or flour. Gently lift the dough onto the center of the parchment, seam side down. Using the parchment as a sling, place it back in the bowl, cover it loosely with plastic wrap and place it in a warm, draft-free spot to rise for another 2 to 3 hours. The dough is ready when it is almost doubled. If you gently poke it with your finger, it should hold the impression. If it doesn't, let it rise for another 15 minutes.

Half an hour before the end of the second rise, preheat the oven to 450°F (230°C), with a rack in the lower middle position and place a covered medium Dutch oven on it.

Using pot holders, carefully remove the preheated pot from the oven and uncover it. Remove the plastic wrap from the dough, lightly dust the top with flour or bran and use a very sharp knife to cut a few slashes into the top. Working quickly, drop 2 to 3 ice cubes into the pot, and then use the parchment as a sling again and place it, with the dough inside, into the pot. (Be careful, the pot will be very hot.) Cover with the lid and bake for 30 minutes. Remove the lid and bake until the bread is deep chestnut brown, 15 to 30 minutes more. Cool on a rack, and then peel the parchment paper off the bottom.

NO-KNEAD CHEDDAR-JALAPEÑO BREAD

Cheddar cheese and jalapeño peppers have always been great partners—in nachos, jalapeño poppers, spicy chile dips—so who are we to deny them their delicious love affair? They go together, in fact, like bread and butter, which is why this recipe works so well. This variation of the no-knead technique uses the addition of good sharp cheddar and chiles with just enough heat to provide a teasing warmth without catching you on fire.

400 g (3¼ cups) all-purpose flour, plus additional for dusting work surface

1 g (⅓ tsp) instant or other active dry yeast

1½ cups minus 1 tbsp (345 ml) lukewarm water (65–72°F [18–22°C])

20 g (1 tbsp) honey

16 g (1 tbsp) fine sea salt

3 jalapeño peppers, seeded, de-ribbed and diced, plus more for decorating, if desired

4 scallions, thinly sliced

170 g (1½ cups [6 oz]) grated sharp cheddar

Wheat bran, cornmeal or additional flour, for dusting

In a large bowl, stir together the flour and yeast. Add the water to a measuring cup or small bowl and stir in the honey and salt until dissolved. Pour the water mixture into the flour and add the jalapeños and scallions. Using your fingers or a wooden spoon, stir until the dough just comes together; it will be craggy and sticky. Cover the bowl with plastic wrap and let it sit at room temperature (about 72°F [22°C]), out of direct sunlight, until the surface is dotted with bubbles and the dough has more than doubled in size. This will take between 12 and (even better) 18 hours. The slower the rise, the more complex the flavor will be. If you want to slow the rise down to suit your baking schedule, you can refrigerate the dough until you're ready for the second rise.

Once the first rise is complete, generously sprinkle a work surface with flour. Use a bowl scraper or rubber spatula to coax the dough out of the bowl. It will be quite loose and sticky, but do not add more flour. Sprinkle the cheddar over and use lightly floured hands or a bowl scraper to pull the corners of the dough in toward the center, mixing the cheese through the dough and roughly making a ball. Nudge and tuck in the edges to make it round.

Place a large piece of parchment paper next to the dough and generously dust it with wheat bran, cornmeal or flour. Gently lift the dough onto the center of the parchment, seam side down. Using the parchment as a sling, place it back in the bowl, cover it loosely with plastic wrap and place it in a warm, draft-free spot to rise for another 2 to 3 hours. The dough is ready when it is almost doubled. If you gently poke it with your finger, it should hold the impression. If it doesn't, let it rise for another 15 minutes.

Half an hour before the end of the second rise, preheat the oven to 450°F (230°C), with a rack in the lower-middle position, and place a covered medium Dutch oven on it.

Using pot holders, carefully remove the preheated pot from the oven and uncover it. Remove the plastic wrap from the dough, lightly dust the top with flour or bran and use a very sharp knife to cut a few slashes into the top. Use the parchment as a sling again and place it, with the dough inside, into the pot. (Be careful, the pot will be very hot.) Cover with the lid and bake for 30 minutes. Remove the lid and bake until the bread is deep chestnut brown, 15 to 30 minutes more. Cool on a rack, and then peel the parchment paper off the bottom.

OLIVE AND ROASTED GARLIC PULL-APART FOCACCIA

There's a reason why focaccia is often the first type of bread most people attempt to bake. It's a simple, forgiving dough, and one that takes extremely well to flavor experimentation. Briny olives give our loaf a salty kick, and since we like ours extra garlicky, we stud the dough with cloves of roasted garlic and, after baking, brush on loads of garlic butter. While you don't have to break the dough into pull-apart sections, it's a fun way to portion it out. Vampires, beware!

Preheat the oven to 350°F (180°C).

To make the garlic, cut off the very top of the heads of garlic so the cloves are exposed. Place the heads in the center of a sheet of aluminum foil. Drizzle with the olive oil and season lightly with salt. Wrap the foil tightly, sealing the garlic in, and place in the oven until the garlic is completely tender, about 1 hour. Allow the garlic to cool completely before opening the foil. Set aside.

To make the focaccia, combine the flour, salt, yeast, water and 3 tablespoons (45 ml) of olive oil in a very large bowl. Mix it with a wooden spoon until no dry flour remains. Cover the bowl tightly with plastic wrap and let it rest in the refrigerator until it doubles in size, 12 to 18 hours. While the dough is resting, peel the roasted garlic cloves and break up any large cloves into two or three pieces. Add the remaining olive oil to a large Dutch oven. Dust your work surface with a little flour and tip the dough out onto it. Using a dough scraper or sharp knife, cut the dough into eight even pieces. Scatter the roasted garlic cloves and the olives evenly over the dough pieces and push them down so they stay evenly distributed, and then shape each piece into a ball. Place one ball in the pot, turn it to coat it in the oil and repeat with the rest of the dough balls.

Cover the pot with the lid and let the dough rest at room temperature for 2 hours. After the first 90 minutes, preheat the oven to 500°F (260°C) and make sure the rack is in the middle. At the end of the 2 hours, the dough should have doubled in size again. Transfer the pot to the oven and bake, uncovered, until the top is golden brown and the bottom is crisp when you lift it with a thin spatula, 18 to 25 minutes.

Meanwhile, make the garlic butter. Add the garlic, olive oil and butter to a small skillet and turn the heat to medium-low. Cook, stirring, until the butter melts and the garlic is fragrant and just beginning to turn golden, 1 to 2 minutes. Scrape into a small bowl, stir in the parsley and season with salt. When the focaccia has finished baking, generously brush the garlic butter over the top.

FOR THE GARLIC HEADS

2 whole heads garlic

15 ml (1 tbsp) extra-virgin olive oil

Kosher salt, as needed

FOR THE FOCACCIA

500 g (4⅛ cups) all-purpose flour, plus additional for dusting

6 g (2 tsp) kosher salt

3 g (1 tsp) instant yeast

1½ cups minus 2 tbsp (330 ml) lukewarm water (70–80°F [21–26°C])

105 ml (7 tbsp) extra-virgin olive oil, divided

100 g (½ cup) kalamata olives, pitted, cut in half

FOR THE GARLIC BUTTER

3 large cloves garlic, minced

15 ml (1 tbsp) extra-virgin olive oil

30 g (2 tbsp) unsalted butter

8 g (2 tbsp) chopped fresh parsley

¼ tsp kosher salt

BEER, HONEY AND SESAME SEED BREAD

People have been baking and brewing from their cereal crops for about as long as we've been farming. Add honey, the original sweetener, and you have a bread that could have been made any time in the last 10,000 years. Using a brown ale and a little honey gives this loaf a lightly malted sweetness.

First, autolyze the dough: Add the flour and beer to a large bowl, and mix with a spoon roughly to combine. Make sure there are no sections of dry flour. Cover with plastic wrap and leave it at room temperature for at least 30 minutes and up to 2 hours.

After the autolysis, add the dough mixture to the bowl of a stand mixer with the dough hook attached and start stirring it at low speed. Add the honey and sprinkle the yeast over, and mix until combined. Add the salt and recombine. Turn the mixer on medium-low and knead the dough until it becomes smooth and elastic. This could take between 5 and 10 minutes. Don't mix for more than 10 minutes or you'll overwork it. Cover the bowl with plastic wrap and let it sit at room temperature (about 72°F [22°C]), out of direct sunlight, until the surface is dotted with bubbles and the dough has more than doubled in size. This may take up to 1 hour but check after 30 minutes.

Generously sprinkle a work surface with flour. Use a bowl scraper or rubber spatula to coax the dough out of the bowl. It may be quite loose and sticky, but do not add more flour. Use lightly floured hands or a bowl scraper to pull the corners of the dough in toward the center, roughly making a ball. Nudge and tuck in the edges to make it round.

At this point, prepare your oven: Adjust the oven rack to the second-lowest position, place a large Dutch oven inside with the lid on and preheat the oven to 475°F (245°C).

Place a large piece of parchment paper next to the dough and generously dust it with flour. Gently lift the dough onto the center of the parchment, seam side down. Using the parchment as a sling, place it back in the bowl, cover it loosely with plastic wrap and place it in a warm, draft-free spot to rise until it has doubled in size again, 30 minutes to 1 hour. If you gently poke it with your finger, it should hold the impression. If it doesn't, let it rise for another 15 minutes.

Brush the top of the dough lightly with the egg white, and then sprinkle over the sesame seeds. Use a razor blade or a sharp knife to make one 6-inch (15-cm)-long, ½-inch (1.3-cm)-deep slit along the top of the dough. Carefully remove the pot from the oven and remove the lid. Add the ice cubes to the pot, and then pick up the dough by lifting the parchment overhang and lower it in. Cover the pot and place it back in the oven. Reduce the oven temperature to 400°F (200°C) and bake the bread for 30 minutes. Remove the lid and continue to bake until the loaf is deep brown, 20 to 30 minutes more. Carefully remove the bread from the pot, transfer to a wire rack and let it cool to room temperature.

500 g (4⅛ cups) all-purpose flour, plus additional for dusting work surface

1 (12-oz [350-ml]) beer, room temperature (we used brown ale, and even though any flavorful beer will work, don't use a beer with alcohol higher than about 8 percent)

40 g (2 tbsp) honey

7 g (2¼ tsp) instant yeast (see Note)

6 g (2 tsp) kosher salt

1 egg white

17 g (2 tbsp) black, white or a mix of sesame seeds

2–3 ice cubes

NOTE: Unlike active dry yeast, instant yeast does not need to be bloomed in liquid. If you have active dry yeast, pour the room-temperature beer into a small measuring cup and sprinkle the yeast over it. Gently stir it in and let the yeast bloom until it turns foamy, about 5 minutes.

For all the same reasons we've talked about in other chapters, a large Dutch oven makes for an excellent deep fryer. Unlike some low and slow techniques (such as braising), deep frying is a fast, technical, hands-on process that has to be managed with care throughout. We think it's worth the effort, as the difference between "oven-fried" potatoes and real Pommes Frites with Three Dipping Sauces (page 135) is night and day. (Don't get us wrong, we make oven fries all the time and love them, but sometimes you just want the real thing.)

Whatever you're frying, the goal is to end up with something that's perfectly cooked on the inside with a crispy exterior that has almost no residual oil. For all these recipes, we strongly recommend you invest in a good instant-read handheld or (preferably) a clip-on thermometer. A candy thermometer will serve in a pinch. In this chapter especially, always approach the hot Dutch oven with care and a stout pair of oven mitts. It is also useful to have a spider, an inexpensive sieve-like utensil that makes it very easy to move items around in the oil and remove them when they're fully cooked.

Most of the dishes in this chapter are best eaten within a few minutes of coming out of the oil. Just like our Indian-Chinese Sweet and Spicy Fried Cauliflower (page 136)—fry them, toss them with spicy sauce and get them in you.

Conversely, the Krispy Berry-Glazed Donuts (page 143), once glazed, will last a few hours—but honestly, if a plate of fresh donuts lasts more than an hour or two in your house, you are way more disciplined than we are.

POMMES FRITES
WITH THREE DIPPING SAUCES

Is there anything that demonstrates the magic of cooking more than taking a humble potato and turning it into a glorious pile of French fries? Our philosophy is, if we're going to go to the trouble of deep-frying, the result had better be worth it (and yes, these are). Exceptionally crisp on the outside, with a fluffy center, these are the fries we dream about.

To make the curried ketchup sauce, in a medium bowl, stir together the ketchup, curry powder, Worcestershire, honey, cayenne and vinegar until combined. Transfer to a sealable jar or serving bowl and refrigerate until ready to serve.

To make the basil green goddess sauce, add the garlic, scallions and basil to the bowl of a food processor or blender. Pulse 10 to 12 times, until the basil is finely minced. Add the anchovies, yogurt, mayonnaise, lemon juice and zest and process until smooth, about 1 minute. Taste for seasoning and add salt and pepper to taste. Transfer to a sealable jar or serving bowl and refrigerate until ready to serve.

To make the kimchi mayo, in a medium bowl, stir together the mayonnaise, kimchi brine, kimchi, sugar, sesame oil, garlic and scallions until well combined. Refrigerate until ready to use.

To make the fries, have a large bowl of cold water ready. Using a mandoline or a knife, cut the potatoes into sticks about ½ inch (1.3 cm) wide. The exact size is less important than making sure they're cut evenly so they cook at the same rate. Immediately place the cut potatoes into the cold water. Bring the 2 quarts (2 L) of water to a boil in a large Dutch oven over high heat. Add 2 tablespoons (16 g) of the kosher salt, the baking soda and the cut potatoes. Return the water to a boil, reduce to a simmer and cook until the potatoes are just cooked through but still have some resistance when you squish them, about 3 minutes after the water returns to a boil. Drain the potatoes well and gently but thoroughly pat them dry with paper towels. Arrange them on a tray so they don't stick together, and then chill them in the refrigerator for at least 1 hour, uncovered, or for up to 1 day before frying.

Set a rack inside a baking sheet. Once the boiled potatoes are completely chilled, heat the oil or duck fat in a large Dutch oven to 375°F (190°C). (If you don't have a thermometer, you'll know the fat is hot enough when you drop in one potato piece and it bubbles energetically and floats to the surface.) Place a large handful of the potatoes onto a spider or a slotted spoon and gently lower it into the oil. Fry the potatoes, gently moving them around in the oil, until they turn crisp and golden brown, 3 to 5 minutes. Remove them with the spider and place them on a wire rack. Season them immediately with salt and either serve them while you cook the next batch, or keep them on the baking tray in a 250°F (120°C) oven until all the batches are fried. Serve hot with your choice of the dipping sauces, or all of them.

FOR SAUCE 1: CURRIED KETCHUP

1 cup (240 ml) ketchup

4 tsp (8 g) curry powder

2 tsp (30 ml) Worcestershire sauce

2 tsp (10 ml) honey

¼ tsp cayenne pepper

1 tsp cider vinegar

FOR SAUCE 2: BASIL GREEN GODDESS

1 small clove garlic, roughly chopped

3 scallions, roughly chopped

½ cup (12 g) coarsely chopped basil (about 20 large leaves)

2 anchovy filets, roughly chopped

½ cup (120 ml) Greek yogurt

½ cup (120 ml) mayonnaise

1 tbsp (15 ml) lemon juice

1 tsp lemon zest

Kosher salt and freshly ground black pepper, to taste

FOR SAUCE 3: KIMCHI MAYO

1 cup (240 ml) mayonnaise

2 tbsp (30 ml) kimchi brine

½ cup (76 g) drained and finely diced kimchi

1 tsp sugar

1 tbsp (15 ml) toasted sesame oil

1 small clove garlic, grated or minced

2 scallions, white and pale-green parts only, finely chopped

FOR THE FRIES

5 large russet potatoes (about 4 lbs [1.8 kg]), peeled

Cold water, plus 2 qt (2 L) for cooking

¼ cup (32 g) kosher salt, plus more as needed, divided

½ tsp baking soda

4 cups (960 ml) peanut oil, duck fat or vegetable oil

INDIAN-CHINESE SWEET AND SPICY FRIED CAULIFLOWER

Sometimes referred to as gobi Manchurian, the dish has become a staple of Indian-Chinese cuisine. It's also very similar to the lasooni gobi we love to order from our local Indian restaurant, Tanjore. Whatever you call it, it's delicious. The tender cauliflower florets are fried in a light batter. The secret to the sauce is the tamarind, which lends sourness and a smoky, caramel flavor. We employ a few tricks to ensure the batter is super crisp without being at all greasy. We use cornstarch as well as flour, which gives the cauliflower a crunchy, golden-brown shell. The ice-cold vodka in the batter evaporates quickly, which helps create larger bubbles and a crispier crust.

To make the sauce, in a cold medium saucepan, add the oil, garlic and ginger. Turn the heat to medium and cook, stirring, until softened, 2 to 3 minutes. Add the cumin seeds and pepper flakes and cook, stirring constantly, until the spices turn fragrant, 30 seconds to 1 minute. Stir in the ketchup, tamarind paste, sugar and soy sauce. Bring it to a simmer and cook until thickened, 2 to 3 minutes. Stir in the sesame oil and set it aside.

To make the cauliflower, preheat the oven to 250°F (120°C) and place a rack in the middle. Set a rack inside a rimmed baking sheet and set it aside.

Add the oil to a large Dutch oven set over medium heat until a thermometer registers 350°F (180°C).

Meanwhile, add the flour, cornstarch, baking powder and salt to a large bowl and whisk until combined. Stir in the water and vodka and whisk until a smooth batter is formed. If the batter is very thick, add another 1 to 2 tablespoons (15 to 30 ml) of water until it has the consistency of heavy cream.

Gently stir all the cauliflower into the batter until it's fully coated. Working one piece at a time, use tongs or your fingers to lift a floret and allow any excess batter to drip off. Carefully lower it into the hot oil. Repeat with the remaining florets until about half are in the pot. (Be careful not to overcrowd the Dutch oven.) Use a spider or slotted spoon to gently move the pieces around as they fry, until the cauliflower is tender in the center with a crisp, golden-brown shell, 6 to 8 minutes. Move them to the rack inside the rimmed baking sheet and sprinkle immediately with a little salt. Place the tray in the warm oven while you fry the remaining florets. Just before serving, toss the fried cauliflower with the sauce and serve immediately, sprinkled with scallions and cilantro.

NOTE: If you can't find tamarind paste in your local grocery, look for it in Asian or Indian markets, or online. For ease, we like the jarred kind, though it's also sold in blocks or as dried pods.

FOR THE SAUCE

2 tbsp (30 ml) peanut or vegetable oil

4 large cloves garlic, minced or grated

1 tbsp (6 g) peeled and minced or finely grated fresh ginger

1 tsp whole cumin seeds

1 tsp crushed red pepper flakes, plus more as desired

½ cup (120 ml) ketchup

3 tbsp (48 g) tamarind paste (sometimes called concentrate; see Note)

2 tbsp (28 g) palm or brown sugar

1 tbsp (15 ml) soy sauce

1½ tbsp (23 ml) toasted sesame oil

FOR THE CAULIFLOWER

2 qt (2 L) peanut or vegetable oil

½ cup (63 g) all-purpose flour

½ cup (64 g) cornstarch

½ tsp baking powder

2 tsp (6 g) kosher salt, plus more as needed

½ cup (120 ml) cold water, plus more as necessary

½ cup (120 ml) cold vodka

1 head cauliflower, cut into 1" (2.5-cm) florets

2 scallions, thinly sliced on an angle, for garnish

¼ cup (4 g) lightly packed cilantro leaves and tender stems

TEMPURA MISTO
(CRISPY FRIED SHRIMP AND VEGETABLES)

A few techniques will help you get perfect tempura every time: Make the batter at the very last minute, keep it very cold, don't overmix it and lastly, keep the oil temperature steady. As for ingredients, aside from the Japanese staples like sweet potato and squash, we take a fritto misto approach and like to crisp up lemon slices, squash blossoms and herbs when they're in season.

To prepare the shrimp, in a medium bowl, toss the shrimp with the salt and baking soda. Cover with plastic wrap and refrigerate it for at least 15 minutes and up to 1 hour. Press each shrimp flat on a clean work surface, and insert a wooden skewer lengthwise to keep it straight while it cooks. Set a rack in a rimmed baking sheet, cover it with two layers of paper towels and place it next to the stove.

To prepare the vegetables, arrange the squash, eggplant, onion, sweet potato, scallions, squash blossoms, lemon slices and shiso leaves on a tray and set them aside.

If you're making the dipping sauce, add the soy sauce, mirin, rice vinegar, sugar and water to a small bowl and stir until the sugar dissolves. Set aside.

Heat the oil to 365°F (185°C) in a large Dutch oven set over medium heat.

As the oil heats, make the batter. (You don't want to make this batter ahead; it will lose its effervescence.) Sift both flours through a fine-mesh sieve into a medium bowl. Add the salt. Whisk the egg and vodka in a small bowl until completely combined. When the oil reaches about 200°F (95°C), add the club soda to the bowl with the egg and vodka and gently mix it with chopsticks or a fork. Pour the egg mixture into the bowl with the flour and gently mix until just barely combined. Be very careful not to overmix; a few pockets of dry flour are fine.

Dust a thin layer of cornstarch or rice flower over the shrimp, scallions and shiso leaves (this helps the batter stick to the more slippery ingredients). Shake off any excess before dipping them in the batter. Add a few shrimp to the batter and gently mix to coat. Using tongs or your fingers, pick up one shrimp at a time, allow any excess batter to drip off and slowly lower it into the hot oil. Increase the heat as needed to keep the temperature as close to 365°F (185°C) as possible. Using chopsticks or a spider, gently move and turn the shrimp in the oil, until the coating turns puffy, crisp and pale gold, 1 to 3 minutes. Remove to the prepared paper towel–lined rack and sprinkle lightly with salt. Between batches, use a slotted spoon to remove any batter crumbs left in the oil. Repeat with the vegetables, lemon slices and shiso, adding them to the oil a few pieces at a time to keep the oil temperature from dropping too much. For the squash blossoms, hold each one by the stem and gently drag the blossom through the batter, allowing excess to drip off. Fry until crisp, 1 to 2 minutes. Serve the tempura immediately with lemon wedges and the dipping sauce, if using.

FOR THE SHRIMP
12 extra-large or jumbo (U21–25) shrimp, peeled, deveined and tails on

1 tsp kosher salt

¼ tsp baking soda

FOR THE VEGETABLES
½ small butternut or kabocha squash, peeled, seeded and cut into ¼" (6-mm) slices

1 small purple eggplant or 2 Japanese eggplants, cut into ¼" (6-mm) rounds

1 medium red or yellow onion, peeled and cut into ½" (1.3-cm) rings

1 small sweet potato, peeled and cut into ¼" (6-mm) slices

5 scallions, roots and greens trimmed

5 squash blossoms, stamens removed

1 lemon, thinly sliced, plus wedges for serving

5 shiso leaves, plus more for serving (optional, or substitute basil or parsley)

FOR THE DIPPING SAUCE (OPTIONAL)
¼ cup (60 ml) soy sauce

¼ cup (60 ml) mirin

1 tbsp (15 ml) unseasoned rice vinegar

1 tsp sugar

2 tsp (10 ml) water

FOR THE BATTER
2 qt (2 L) peanut oil or vegetable oil

¾ cup (94 g) all-purpose flour

¾ cup (120 g) rice flour or cornstarch, plus more for dusting

1 tsp kosher salt, plus more as needed

1 large egg

½ cup (120 ml) ice-cold vodka

1 cup (240 ml) ice-cold club soda

TALEGGIO-STUFFED ARANCINI
WITH BASIL-CHILI DIPPING SAUCE

Arancini, a Sicilian dish that translates to "little oranges," are stuffed, crispy fried balls of risotto. When oversized, arancini can be disappointingly dry, with none of the melting ooziness that makes risotto so tempting. We prefer to keep their size small and imbue the risotto with a little extra richness. Stuffing them with creamy, tangy taleggio cheese and gooey mozzarella doesn't hurt either. Yes, there's a little bit of a process involved in making them, but we like to think Sicilians would approve.

To make the dipping sauce, in a medium bowl, stir together the basil, mayonnaise and lemon zest. Season with salt and pepper, to taste. Swirl in the chiles, leaving streaks of red in the white sauce. Refrigerate until ready to use.

To make the arancini, place the taleggio cubes onto a tray in a single layer, cover with plastic wrap and refrigerate until you're ready to stuff the rice balls.

Bring the stock to a simmer in a medium pot, and then lower the heat to keep at a bare simmer.

Melt 2 tablespoons (30 g) of the butter in a large Dutch oven set over medium heat. Add the onion and a good pinch of salt and pepper, and cook, stirring often, until softened but not brown, 4 to 5 minutes. Add the garlic and cook, stirring constantly, until the garlic is fragrant, about 1 minute. Stir in the rice and cook, stirring often, until the grains turn translucent around the edges, about 3 minutes. Add the wine and stir until the pan is almost dry, about 2 minutes. Ladle in 1½ cups (360 ml) of the hot stock and cook, stirring often, until the liquid is absorbed, about 4 minutes. Repeat this process until the rice is cooked through but just a little al dente, 15 to 20 minutes. You may not need to add all of the stock.

Remove the pot from the heat and stir in the Parmigiano-Reggiano, cream, lemon zest and the remaining butter. Taste the risotto and season as desired. Stir in 1 beaten egg. Spread the risotto out evenly onto a parchment-lined rimmed baking sheet. Cover the top with plastic wrap and allow it to chill for at least 1½ hours and up to overnight.

(continued)

FOR THE BASIL-CHILI DIPPING SAUCE

½ cup (12 g) packed, chopped basil leaves

1 cup (240 ml) mayonnaise or Greek yogurt

2 tsp (4 g) finely grated lemon zest

Kosher salt and freshly ground black pepper, to taste

1–3 tbsp (15–45 g) minced Calabrian chiles in oil, to taste

FOR THE ARANCINI

6 oz (170 g) taleggio cheese, cut into small cubes (this is easier to do when very cold)

5½ cups (1.3 L) Golden Chicken Stock (page 84) or store-bought stock

¼ cup (56 g) unsalted butter, divided

1 medium onion, very finely chopped

Kosher salt and freshly ground black pepper, as needed

3 medium cloves garlic, minced or grated

2 cups (390 g) carnaroli, arborio or short-grain sushi rice

¾ cup (180 ml) dry white wine

½ cup (50 g) finely grated Parmigiano-Reggiano

¼ cup (60 ml) heavy cream

2 tsp (4 g) finely grated lemon zest

3 large eggs, divided

Line a second rimmed baking sheet with parchment. Remove the taleggio cheese from the refrigerator. Scoop about ¼ cup (50 g) of the risotto into your hands and form a rough patty shape. Place a piece or two of the cheese into the center of the patty, then gently shape the rice into a ball so it completely encases the cheese. Be careful not to overstuff them, and don't worry about making them perfectly round at this point. Place the ball on the prepared baking sheet and repeat with the remaining risotto and cheese. Freeze the balls for at least 10 minutes while you prepare for frying.

If you're using panko (or if your homemade breadcrumbs are large), pulse them in a food processor or place them in a sealable plastic bag and press them with a rolling pin until finer crumbs form. Transfer the crumbs to a shallow bowl. Add the flour to a second shallow bowl. Lightly beat the remaining eggs in a third shallow bowl. Lightly season each bowl with salt and pepper. Working one at a time, dredge the balls in flour, shake off any excess, move them to the bowl with the eggs and turn them all over to coat. Roll the balls in the breadcrumbs, pressing them gently to adhere and gently form them into a rounder shape if needed. Transfer them back to the parchment-lined baking sheet and return them to the refrigerator while you heat the oil.

Add at least 3 inches (8 cm) of oil into a medium or large Dutch oven. Heat over medium heat until a thermometer registers 350°F (180°C). Carefully lower a few rice balls into the oil with a slotted spoon or spider, being careful not to crowd the pot. Fry until they turn deep golden brown, 6 to 8 minutes, adjusting the heat to keep the temperature as close to 350°F (180°C) as you can. Transfer them to paper towels to drain and season immediately with salt. Repeat with the remaining rice balls. Serve the arancini hot, with the dipping sauce and extra lemons for squeezing. The balls can also be allowed to cool, and then stored in the refrigerator. Reheat them on a rimmed baking sheet in a 350°F (180°C) oven until hot.

2 cups (100 g) finely ground homemade breadcrumbs or panko

½ cup (63 g) all-purpose flour

2 qt (2 L) peanut, vegetable or canola oil, for frying

Lemon wedges, for garnish

KRISPY BERRY-GLAZED DONUTS

There's no Krispy Kreme franchise around these parts, so we had to fry up a batch of our own. These light and airy beauties get their ethereal texture from tangzhong, *the yeast technique that makes Japanese milk bread extra soft and pillowy. Don't be tempted to heat your oil too quickly over high heat; heating the pot over medium will make it much easier to maintain the correct oil temperature. These golden-brown, super-crispy donuts are good enough to serve with just a sprinkling of powdered sugar or cinnamon sugar, but we love to coat them in a glaze made with bright, zingy freeze-dried berries.*

FOR THE TANGZHONG (THIS MAKES MORE THAN YOU'LL NEED)

⅓ cup (42 g) all-purpose flour

1 cup (240 ml) water

FOR THE DOUGH

½ cup (120 ml) milk

2¼ tsp (7 g) active dry yeast (1 package)

½ cup (120 ml) tangzhong (see above)

1 large egg, room temperature

½ tsp vanilla extract or paste

2½ cups (313 g) all-purpose flour

1 tbsp (4 g) nonfat dry milk powder

¼ cup (50 g) sugar

½ tsp fine sea salt

¼ tsp freshly grated nutmeg

3 tbsp (42 g) very soft unsalted butter

6 cups (1.4 L) vegetable shortening or vegetable oil, for frying

To make the tangzhong, whisk the flour and water together in a small saucepan until no lumps remain. Place the saucepan over low heat, and cook the mixture, whisking constantly, until it thickens and the whisking starts to reveal the bottom of the pan, 3 to 5 minutes. Transfer the tangzhong to a small mixing bowl or measuring cup, and let it cool to room temperature. Set aside.

To make the dough, add the milk to a small saucepan and heat it over low until it reaches about 110°F (45°C). Pour it into a medium bowl and stir in the yeast. Let it sit until the yeast blooms and turns foamy, 3 to 5 minutes. Measure out ½ cup (120 ml) of the cooled tangzhong and add it, along with the egg and vanilla, to the milk-yeast mixture. Stir until combined. Add the flour, milk powder, sugar, salt and nutmeg to the bowl of a stand mixer fitted with the dough hook and stir to combine. Make a well in the center of the dry ingredients and pour in the milk-tangzhong mixture. Turn the mixer on low and mix until the dough comes together and becomes fairly smooth, about 5 minutes. With the mixer on low, add the butter, 1 tablespoon (15 g) at a time, waiting until each spoonful is fully incorporated before adding the next. Continue to knead on low speed until the dough is smooth and very stretchy, 10 to 15 minutes. Transfer the dough to a greased bowl, turn it over to coat the top, cover and let it rise until it doubles in size, 1½ to 2 hours.

Cut about fifteen 4-inch (10-cm) squares of parchment, lay them out in a single layer on a large baking sheet and set aside. Turn the dough out onto a lightly floured surface and gently roll it out to ¼ to ½ inch (6 to 13 mm) thick. Cut out the donuts using a lightly floured 3-inch (8-cm) round cutter, and then use a smaller 1-inch (2.5-cm) cutter for the middle, re-rolling the scraps as necessary. (Alternatively, use a sharp donut cutter.) Keep the holes if you want to fry them. Place each donut on one square of parchment. When all the donuts have been cut out, cover the baking sheet loosely with plastic wrap, and allow the donuts to rise at room temperature for 1 hour.

(continued)

KRISPY BERRY-GLAZED DONUTS (CONTINUED)

About 20 minutes before the donuts have finished rising, heat the shortening or oil in a large Dutch oven, set over medium heat, to 365°F (185°C). Set a wire rack inside a rimmed baking sheet, and set it next to the stove. Gently lower one donut with its parchment square into the hot oil. The parchment will dislodge; use tongs to remove it. Repeat with two or three more donuts, adjusting the temperature under the oil as needed to keep it between 350°F and 365°F (180°C and 185°C). Cook the donuts until they are golden brown on one side, 1 minute to 90 seconds, and then flip and cook the other side for about 1 minute. (The internal temperature of the donuts should be about 200°F [95°C] when fully cooked.) Remove the donuts with a spider or a slotted spoon to the wire rack and repeat with the remaining dough, working in batches, as needed. Fry the holes last.

To make the glaze, add the confectioners' sugar and freeze-dried berries to a food processor and process until it becomes a fine powder. Sift the powder through a fine-mesh sieve into a wide, shallow bowl, discarding any seeds, and add the cream, vanilla and salt. Mix until it becomes smooth. Stir in more cream or water, as needed, until the glaze is thin enough to drizzle. Dunk the tops of the warm donuts into the glaze, or drizzle over the glaze with a spoon and return them to the wire rack to set. Decorate with crushed freeze-dried berries or sprinkles, if using, while the glaze is still runny.

FOR THE GLAZE

1 cup (120 g) confectioners' sugar

1 cup (30 g) freeze-dried berries (blueberry, blackberry, strawberry or raspberry), plus more for decorating

¼ cup (60 ml) heavy cream, plus more as needed

1 tsp vanilla extract or paste

¼ tsp fine sea salt

Sprinkles (optional)

PEAR FRITTERS
WITH LEMON-GINGER GLAZE

Fritters are like donuts' freewheeling, devil-may-care cousin. While donuts come in one shape (round), fritters are craggy, spiky and full of character (just like us!). Apples tend to be the choice for frittering around here, but we like to mix it up and use pears, with their delicate, floral sweetness. The variety of pear you use matters: Bosc and Anjou varieties hold their shape when cooked, which is important if you want little bits of pear scattered throughout the fritter. (You do!) Top them off with a light lemony glaze, flecked with spicy flecks of candied ginger . . . you won't regret it.

To make the fritters, in a medium bowl, whisk together the flour, baking powder, salt and ground ginger. In a separate bowl, combine the lemon juice, lemon zest and diced pears. In the bowl of a stand mixer fitted with the paddle attachment (or use a bowl and a handheld beater), beat the sugar and eggs on medium speed until fully combined and foamy. Reduce the speed to low and add half of the flour mixture. Beat until it's just combined; a few streaks of flour are fine. Repeat with the second half of the flour mixture. With the speed on low, slowly pour in the milk and mix until just incorporated. Remove the bowl from the mixer and fold in the pear mixture with a silicone spatula.

Heat 1½ inches (4 cm) of the oil to 350°F (180°C) in a large Dutch oven set over medium heat. Set a rack in a rimmed baking sheet, cover with two layers of paper towels and place it next to the stove. Use a portion scoop or measuring cup to carefully drop ¼-cup (60-ml) batches of batter into the oil. Repeat two or three more times, but don't overcrowd the pot. Fry until the fritters turn golden brown on the bottom. Flip and fry until the other sides are golden brown, 2 to 3 minutes per side. To test for doneness, insert a skewer or small knife into the center. If there's still wet batter in the center, continue to fry a little longer. Use a spider or a slotted spoon to transfer the fritters to the rack. Repeat with the remaining batter.

To make the glaze, add the confectioners' sugar to a bowl and stir in 2 tablespoons (30 ml) of lemon juice. If the glaze is too thick to drizzle off a spoon, add more lemon juice until it's the right consistency. Let the fritters cool slightly, and then use a spoon to drizzle the glaze over the tops of each fritter. Sprinkle a little candied ginger over the glaze.

FOR THE FRITTERS

1½ cups (188 g) all-purpose flour

2 tsp (9 g) baking powder

½ tsp kosher salt

½ tsp ground ginger

2 tsp (10 ml) fresh lemon juice

2 tsp (4 g) finely grated lemon zest

2–3 Bosc or Anjou pears, peeled, cored and finely diced (about 2½ cups [400 g])

3 tbsp (39 g) sugar

2 large eggs, room temperature

⅔ cup (160 ml) whole milk

About 2 qt (2 L) vegetable shortening or canola oil

FOR THE GLAZE

2 cups (240 g) sifted confectioners' sugar

2–3 tbsp (30–45 ml) lemon juice

2 tbsp (10 g) very finely minced candied ginger

THANK YOUS

For this book, we approached a number of Dutch oven manufacturers to ask if they would send us ovens that we could use to test our recipes in various sizes and shapes, and to our surprise and delight, they did! We especially want to thank Great Jones, Le Creuset and Emile Henry, whose marvelous ovens, among others, you will see scattered throughout this book. We also want to thank Lisa Hall and Chris Pascarella, the butchers at Marbled Meat of Cold Spring, NY, who sourced a lot of the meat we cooked (at generously low cost). It's always worth building a relationship with your local butcher, who can often be a great source of information on cooking as well as a valued resource for quality cuts of meat.

This book was written throughout the spring and summer of 2020, and it would be odd not to mention the virus that brought the planet to a near standstill. We were fortunate that our friends and family remained healthy, but the effects touched everyone. We want to thank all the essential workers who risked their lives to save ours, who kept the world spinning and the shelves stocked. We especially want to thank the workers at Adams Fairacre Farms, and all of our local farms, for keeping on when things were hardest.

Closer to home, we had planned a major kitchen renovation to be completed by April 2020. This was to be the kitchen of our dreams, a long-awaited transformation of a bare-bones utilitarian cooking space into an efficient and beautiful room that would accommodate both family cooking and blog work. Our timing couldn't have been worse: We ripped out our old kitchen cabinets at the beginning of March, days before New York was totally shut down. It was a month before we even had a temporary utility sink installed (that's a long time to be handwashing dishes in the bathroom vanity), another two months before we had lighting put into the ceiling and another three months before we had new kitchen cabinets installed. In the space of those six months, this book was planned, cooked for and photographed, entirely in the renovation chaos.

For much of that time, health advisories prevented us from seeing family or friends. Friends came anyway, leaving food and supplies when we were at our lowest ebb, helping us clean and organize and do dishes when we hadn't the energy to cope. We're looking at you, Catherine and Larry. Our friend, neighbor and brilliant photographer, Eva Deitch, kindly lent us her lighting kit for the duration of the photography—Eva, thank you. You saved the book.

During this turbulent time, podcasts helped us keep our sanity. Among others, we want to note our appreciation for the talents of Karen Kilgariff and Georgia Hardstark at *My Favorite Murder* and Eric Molinsky at *Imaginary Worlds*.

Thanks to the team at Page Street Publishing for their continuing faith in us and their hard work in getting the book to press.

To friends who extended invites to gatherings that we had to regretfully turn down: thank you. We can't wait to hug you. To friends who phoned just to tell us they loved us: thank you. We love you, too.

As always, we're grateful to the readers of our blog, Nerds with Knives, and our previous cookbook, *Cork and Knife*, for sending us feedback and photos of your versions of the recipes, and for all your love and appreciation. It means the world.

ABOUT THE AUTHORS

Emily's culinary adventures began on the gritty streets of 1970s Manhattan, where she ate Pernil and kimchi more often than peanut butter and jelly. Now she develops recipes that combine locally sourced ingredients into simple but delicious dishes. When she's not cooking, writing or taking photographs of radish tops, she's probably hard at work editing a movie or television show, which she's done professionally for the last twenty years.

Matt grew up in Kent, England, and his upbringing involved a suspiciously large proportion of tinned goods. (Many of those tins contained sticky toffee pudding, though, so it really wasn't all that bad.) When he's not thinking about food, he's running an IT consultancy or cursing at his vegetable garden. At the very moment you're reading this, there's a good chance he's chasing one or all of his chickens back into the yard.

Together they cowrite the cookery blog Nerds with Knives, and their first cookbook, *Cork and Knife*, was published in 2019. They live in the Hudson Valley of New York.

INDEX